MW00635429

FROM THE VISIONARY

Foreword

DEBBIE
LESEAN

Debbie LeSean is THE Coach to call when you're ready to turn turmoil into triumph. Debbie is focused on helping women embrace the rain, celebrate the rainbow then be the sun in another woman's storm by sharing their story. Her God-given assignment is to help women heal their heart and master their emotions with the use of a pen. Her job is to reframe limiting beliefs, eliminate doubt, and provide customized techniques on inking their way to victory.

Debbie holds a B.S. from VCU & an M.A. in Counseling from Liberty University. She credits the streets of New York with teaching her life skills that a classroom could not.

Follow her on coachdebbielesean f debbielesean
or check out her website at www.**debbielesean.com**

I remember it like it was yesterday. I was so depressed thinking my life was over. I was facing divorce for the second time and I was so embarrassed. I'm a leader and I fix problems. What was wrong with me that I couldn't fix my marriage. I was a failure, my relationship was a failure, I had more debt than income, this really could not be my life. But there I was. Broke, divorced, and wondering "Why Me ?!?" I didn't know that God was using that situation to get me ready. It was time to push!

Let me clarify. This book is not about childbirth but rather about birthing your God-given purpose. Every one of us are impregnated with a gift that only you have. For many of us, we walk around with this gift but we never birth it; we simply don't use it. There are many reasons why we don't birth our purpose. In my opinion, the biggest reason is because we get caught up in survival mode. You know that mode where we go to work every day, take care of children, manage the household, and wear all the hats that women wear. I lived that way for over 35 years. Who knew that I/we was created for so much more than survival mode.

There are times God will stir things up. A friend will cross you, a death may happen, divorce may blindside you. It's all part of God's birthing plan. God uses heartaches and traumas to force us to change. For me, he used my embarrassment, my heartbreak, my financial woes to push me. If I had my way, I would still be at my former place of employment, with great friends, financially responsible for myself, and floating through life. God said, "No

Ma'am!" During this time, God pushed, I cried and fought against it until I finally said "God you win. What is it I'm supposed to be doing with my life right now?" During my quiet time of emotional healing, I learned that this gift is much bigger than me/us. We were created on purpose, to operate with purpose and to operate in our purpose. Let me help you understand. Birthing your purpose is no easy task. It is almost like childbirth, thus the title "It's Time to Push." Have you had enough of walking around with your supernatural gift inside you? Are you ready to use it? Are you saying, "Coach, how do I birth my gift?"

Ask any woman who has been pregnant and had a vaginal birth. It takes a bit of strenuous pushing. You have to help your gift be born by pushing. Pushing past fear, past doubt, past insecurities, past financial challenges, past your comfort zone and more. It may seem that as soon as you push past one challenge and catch your breath, here comes something else. Just like childbirth! There's a well-defined rest period, but contractions come back- to-back. Well, that was the experience with my 2 children. God is stirring some things up in your life and pushing you into your purpose.

Here are some tips I've come up with to help push out your purpose:
Get into pushing position. To get into your pushing position, get comfortable on your knees with your face to the floor. It is the position of prayer, submission and humility. I spent so much time in prayer as I pushed out my purpose. I had to learn me, my strengths, my weaknesses, my personality and more. I prayed so hard and questioned God. There had to be a mistake.

The more I got quiet, the clearer my directives were. Spending time in the push/prayer position allowed me to LISTEN. I have a solution for everything, but not this time. It was meant for me to be quiet, listen and learn.

Be encouraged. God will not push you into position until a new door is opening. Walking into anything new can be nerve wracking and may make you want to revert to your old, comfortable zone. In your comfort zone, there's peace because you know what to expect. With a new purpose, you are walking into the unknown. There's no growth in your comfort zone. It's one thing to walk aimlessly into the unknown. It's another thing to walk knowing that an open door is there, just keep going. One leads to frustration, the other is exciting. Which direction are you walking in? Get help!

Whether you have your baby at home or in a hospital, there is someone assigned to help you. The same happens when you are birthing your purpose. God will send you help. It's up to you to recognize it and accept it. Stinking thinking is real. It takes on the form of self-doubt, competition, jealousy, fear and more. Having someone to help coach you through the pushing process is invaluable. Find someone trustworthy, someone who has been where you're trying to go, someone who can pray with and for you, someone who will grab your hand and say, "Sis, it's time to push!" **Enjoy the book,**

Debbie

Before Starting This Book, Will You Say This With Me:

I'm Ready & Open to the Blooming Process.

Allow Yourself to be Pruned of limiting **THOUGHTS**,

Uprooted from your comfort zone, and

REPLANTED so you can bloom how GOD intended.

Now, It's Time to **PUSH!**

TABLE OF

Contents

BECOMING THE

Lighthouse

CHAPTER

CHRISTINA
NICOLE

Christina-Nicole is a woman who wears many titles: mother, daughter, sister, business owner, mentor and so many more. She is a woman who truly believes in the power of prayer. Her passions in life are cooking, her kids and helping women to love themselves truly. On her journey of self-discovery God showed her how to fuse both her passions for cooking and helping broken women become whole again. Christina-Nicole is a woman on a mission to grow and during the process, committed to being open and transparent to other women along the way. This is her first published anthology and she is looking forward to having more projects to come.

Follow her on 📷 @christinanicolespeaks 📘 Christina-Nicole's Culinary Creations
or check out her website at www.CNicoleEvents.com

BECOMING THE
lighthouse

Definition of a Lighthouse: a tower or other structure containing a beacon of light to warn or guide ships at sea. (per Google definition)

What is the purpose of the lighthouse? It is a tower with a bright light at the top, located at an important or dangerous place regarding navigation (travel over water). Now you might ask why I have listed the definition and purpose of something that you may never see on a daily basis. The lighthouse is most needed during the darkest stormy hour.

Watching someone else go through their personal tragedy and you experiencing your own personal tragedy are two completely different things. It is also one thing to go through something so detrimental in private and another for it to be blasted in a public way. Have you ever heard someone say to you "Couldn't have been me" or "Girl you are better than me"? It is in these moments that you, my sister, are becoming the lighthouse. You are being erected to fight a storm and lead the pathway for others to follow. The journey to becoming the lighthouse is one that is dark and possibly the most shameful thing that you will experience. For it is in the middle of tragedy that greatness is born. I know that was the case for me.

It was within year twelve, I realized my biggest fear was coming to life. I was becoming a single mom of four kids and a statistic. I was married for 13 years and they were some of the most painful years of my life. Before you think wrong, yes, there were also good years but the ending darkens my view of my entire marriage. When you get married there are so many hopes and dreams for the future. The hopes of having a family then, finding the best home to raise them, obtaining the perfect job, the family vehicle, and more. You start living out your dreams with the focus of making them a reality with the one person you love more than life itself. Just typing this helped me realize that the biggest mistake I ever made was putting my husband on a pedestal higher than God. God knocked my ex off the pedestal and showed me the correct family order. Once I knew how it was supposed to be, my life and focus changed drastically, forever.

Please understand that in no way am I saying that marriage is bad that is not my point at all. I want to be married again, but this time to the man God has for me and not a man I choose. Marriage is a beautiful thing and it should be cherished as such. Friendship is such an important factor in your marriage. My tragedy was something that was public in the world we made. It was something that I could no longer hide from. While I was hiding, it was only being brought to the forefront by his actions. God has a funny way of getting your attention. As I was going through my personal hell, my sister was my lighthouse. She was the one that I confided in and wept on her shoulders. Same as I had for her when she was going through her first marriage and divorce. She was my beacon of strength and also my mirror that I couldn't lie to because she had been in my shoes. The phrase misery loves company is a total lie. In my time of misery, I wanted to be left alone and not be bothered with anyone or anything. I felt as if the weight of the world was on my shoulders. I was going through the motions of life but I wasn't truly living at all. The only thing that brought me any joy were my kids and I absolutely had no energy for them. To say that I was on autopilot was a true understatement. The hardest thing that I had to accept was the fact that I had lost myself and had no idea who I was anymore. I had so many hopes and dreams for myself and my family. I hadn't looked in a mirror in a long time. I am 5'2". At my lowest point in my life, I was weighing almost 250 pounds. I was a size 22 and life was bad.

I was silently crying out for help. I am forever grateful for my sister knowing and understanding me, so she knew I was silently pleading for help. As I was going through my personal hell. God was sending women to me who were going through very similar journeys. I was like really God? How can I offer any advice to these women when my life was in a total disarray? I was trying to find myself and keep my own life afloat. I was losing so much and drowning in my own pain. However, it was something in me that kept forcing me to move forward. To keep forging the sea of life. When I thought the waves would take me under something would allow me to ride the wave and take a deep breathe while I was being held under. As beautiful as the ocean is on the surface, she is a dangerous beast under the surface. She will trick you into thinking that you are floating along, then out of nowhere a strong wave will knock you out the boat. You will be so blindsided; you will be caught out there without a life preserver or even a rowboat. The water is not the only worry you should have. There are sharks in the water girlfriend. They come in the shape of bills piling up, wayward kids, family leaving you, folks talking about you and sinking you all while all you're trying to stay afloat.

My advice for you: do not be afraid to travel the road or navigate the waters. I honestly thought I would not be able to get past the shame of my ex-husband's infidelity and having an outside baby. I just knew that it was over for me. I was ashamed of how people would look at me. The crazy thing is that the baby was not the end of his cheating. Cheating became a constant part of our marriage. It was the dark and shark infested waves I simply could not seem to ride. It was always taking me under and making me feel like I was drowning in shame. Something that I wanted to keep to myself became very hard when he kept putting it on display for everyone to see. He wasn't worried about anyone but himself. I never had negative feelings toward the child he did nothing to me. He is honestly my bonus baby. I love him and have helped take care of him.

He is a sweetie pie and I have enjoyed my time with him. I would have thought my ex-husband tighten up and focus on family, but he did not. However, things began to shift. I changed my prayer from God fix him to God fix me. It was at that moment I questioned why don't I love my own self anymore?

On this journey of coming into your purpose you will have people watching you that you never thought. I can laugh at this now because I'm out of my darkest moment. I recall the first Christmas after of my divorce. I have 4 kids and at the time my oldest was 12 years old and my youngest was only 2 years old. My sister said that we were going to spend the holiday with them. I wasn't even thinking about Christmas (which is my favorite holiday besides Easter). We had been evicted from the house we were renting because he stopped paying the rent. With the help of my job and sister I was able to move into a new place and different county which brought on a new set of battles. That is a story for another time. I received a call from a lady on Christmas Eve to apologize for her lateness.

Mind you I had no idea who this woman was or what she wanted from me. She was out of breath, stating she had just gotten back in town and that she needed to see me ASAP to help me with Christmas gifts for my kids. I was taken aback because again I had no idea how she knew me or anything let alone had my phone number. She went on to say that she received my information from a woman who knew me and felt like I needed some help. All I could do was cry and thank God for the blessing. She met with me that night at my sister's house. I really wanted her to tell me who had recommended me. I wanted to say thank you at least. When she told me the name I was totally amazed because this wasn't a person that I saw on a daily basis or even talked with to share my story. Turns out, the woman attended church with me. When I saw this woman in church the following Sunday, I walked up to her and just hugged her. She whispered in my ear "I have been seeing how you're handling everything with such grace and you are an inspiration to me". When I say we hugged each other tighter and just cried, girl it was ugly! It was something that I will always remember because it was confirmation to me that I was on the right path and that I was doing the correct thing. When I finally accepted the fact that I was not the one in control my life, my journey changed. I was no longer fighting the water but learning how to read the currents. I was learning when to breathe and when to exhale. I was understanding that not every wave was meant to kill me but to teach me and purify me. It is a journey that I am still on right now. Now the waves do not scare me as much. I am at the point where I realize that I am here to show other women that even though they may be in some deep, dark water they can make it out also. I have realized my purpose and in that I am on a different journey through life. It took the process of understanding that the "old" Christina was dead. I had to learn the "NEW" Christina. I had to learn to love her bruises and scars. At first, I looked at them as something ugly. This journey has allowed me to see the beauty of what they truly are. They are reminders of the things that tried to take me out. The bible says that the weapons will form but they won't prosper. I have had weapons thrown at me that I did not even know existed. Weapons come in many forms so always be on the lookout. They do not always look like what you think they are supposed to be.

Do I get weary? Yes, I do. Are some days harder than others? YES GOD!! What keeps me going is that I am closer to my destiny than I was seven years ago when I got divorced. I am walking into a blessing that is going to bring more joy than I ever imagined. The biggest take away I have learned is that if I do not take my place and accept my purpose than there are people who will not get their blessing. I do not want to die and stand before God stating that I was afraid to live on purpose. Just think if you don't live on purpose and share your story, someone could miss out on their blessing. Sounds crazy but it is so true. I know that is not something that I want on my hands. I do not take becoming the lighthouse lightly. To be a lighthouse you are visible and on display. To have your wounds and battle scars visible to anyone and everyone. To be on constant display when sometimes all you want is to hide and just have a moment of peace or just be able to cry without an audience. To be called up to shine a light on someone who is drowning and show them a way when you are not sure of your own pathway sometimes. To be looked at as a beacon, a safe place and confidant. When the waves of life are thrashing all around you and you are looking to be saved instead, you are supposed to save someone else. These things can become overwhelming but you can't let it overtake you. Sometimes you just have to be your own lighthouse. My saving grace throughout all of this has been journaling. When I go back and read over the trials and things that I have come through, it keeps me going. These are things that I did not think I would survive. My personal motto is "Trusting the process". The "ING" makes it a verb which is an action. I am doing the action of TRUSTING. It is something that I do actively every day. When I knew my purpose was to help women this became my focus point as I speak to women. We are called to action on different levels and each level will require more of you. The change was amazing because it was in that time that I was spending more time getting to know myself for myself. I was no longer able to run from my destiny. I was no longer hiding from my fears but taking them head on. Fighting the battle of my mind and allowing myself to stand securely on my faith and trusting that God had my best interest at heart for me and my babies. I wanted to show my babies what real love is and it always starts with YOU.

I started playing music in my house and dancing with my babies. I simply started loving Christina and enjoying the power that she held. I have lost weight and gained my genuine smile back. Before, I would not be in pictures now you cannot keep me out the camera. Selfie, yes ma'am!! I have a wall of my favorite selfies and my family pictures to be a constant reminder of why I have made the choices I have. You must know your why, it is what will keep you swimming though the rough waters of life when you get tired and ready to give up. Know my sister that is okay to turn on your back and float sometimes just don't stay there. It is a necessity to learn to swim and navigate the waters. I will be there guiding the way as I shine my light as a guide to let you know that it is possible just keep moving. Never give up and never stop swimming. The waves are temporary but the current is always moving and that is the promise of growth. Just make me a promise that as I light your way you will turn on your light and shine it in complete transparency to light the way for someone else who may be waiting on a sign as well. In closing for me music has been a "lighthouse". I have decided to share some of the songs that helped me along the way. I hope that they speak to you also.

PLAYLIST

K'Jon—On the Ocean

Katy Perry -ROAR

Vedo-You Got it

Fantasia—Lose to Win

Estelle—Conqueror

Chris Brown—Zero

Leon Bridges—River

Anita Baker—Fairytales

Goapele—Closer

Donald Lawrence & the Tri-City

Singers—Deliver Me

Jill Scott—Closure

Andra Day—Rise Up

K.Michelle –Cry

Fantasia—I'm Doin Me

Leela James—Don't want you back

Kevin LeVar—Here I am

Jessica Reedy—Better

Kelly Price—Tired

Ciara—Level Up

William McDowell—Not going back

Tasha Cobbs—For your glory

Tasha Cobbs—Break every chain

Keyshia Cole – Every album she ever made. LOL

Acknowledgements

To my mother, Bonnie Taylor who in her own way made me fearless and allowed me to know that the world isn't always a pretty place. You were my safe haven. You are forever my rose and you bloom beautifully in my garden.

To my godmother who is no longer with me, Angel Faria. You were my second mother and the one who gave me my passion for cooking. You were a fearless woman who broke the rules and dared to love against all the odds.

To my village… I LOVE YOU ALL!! You have carried me in prayer and for that I am eternally grateful.

To my sister, Tonja Wright, there are no words that will ever be able to express my love for you. You are and will forever be my best friend, sister, ride or die and the one who I can truly always be myself with.

To my children, Alana, Azaria, Andrea and Zion, I pray that I am raising you all right. I pray that you all are able to love and accept nothing less than what you deserve. I am so honored to be your mother. Thank you for the days you kept me smiling when all I wanted to do was laydown and die. Y'all have kept me in more ways than you will ever know. On my darkest days y'all always provided a reason for me to smile and find joy in my heart.

To my ex-husband, in so many ways you have helped me become the woman I was always meant to be. Thank you for the role that you had to play for me to learn the lessons that I needed to learn.

To my future husband and stepfather to my children, I pray that you are mentally well and know that I can't wait for the day God brings us together. You are not in my life at this moment, but I know you are on the way. It is going to be beautiful.

Dedication

I want to dedicate this chapter to every woman who has ever felt herself drowning. To every woman who felt that she had to make herself small just so that others around her could feel bigger than what they truly were. To every woman who is fearful of success and operating in their true purpose. To the woman who is a GIANT in spirit but feels smaller than an ant in the flesh. To the woman who is afraid to keep living like she is and knows that better is out there but that means breaking the status quo. Ladies, this chapter is for you. I have lit the pathway; all you have to do is take the first step and keep moving forward.

Reflections

_____

_____

_____

_____

_____

_____

_____

_____

_____

_____

_____

_____

_____

_____

_____

_____

_____

_____

Reflections

TO PRESTON, WITH LOVE:

Labor Pains

CHAPTER

SHEREE

WONG

Sheree E. Wong affectionately, known as Sher by her close friends and family is a lifelong educator. Ms. Wong holds a Post-Master's certificate in Administration and Leadership, from The George Washington University. She holds an Educational Specialist degree in Administration and Leadership and a Master's degree in Curriculum, Instruction, and Assessment from Walden University. She also holds a Bachelor of Science degree in Elementary Education from Long Island University, C.W. Post campus. She holds certifications in the areas of elementary education, gifted education, and administration and leadership. Sheree possesses over nineteen plus years in the field of education. She has taught every grade at the elementary level, with the exception of fourth grade. Currently, Sheree serves as the Dean of Goshen Post Elementary School, which is located in Aldie, Virginia. Sheree enjoys spending time with her friends and family, event planning, and serving in her community.

Follow her on @authorengelle ShereeWong

First Trimester of

Pain

August 02, 2008 was a regular day, until it wasn't. As I woke up and saw blood while using the bathroom, one thing was clear, pain. Sharp, visceral, emotional, raw, unyielding pain. I was twenty weeks pregnant with my son, my first child and when I woke up I knew, I would never experience the joy of holding, and caring for my son. I could handle the physical pain, however, as I write all these years later, I continue to struggle with the emotional pain of losing my boy. My son, **Preston**.

I woke up in the morning in extreme pain. I looked at my then-husband with tears in my eyes as my worst fears were beginning to come true. I got myself together and prepared to go to work. When I arrived at work the tears began to stream down my face as I was in tremendous pain. My principal and the front office secretaries could see the pain not only in my face but within my body and immediately sent me home. I called my husband and he picked me up and we began our trip to the doctor. As I walked into the doctor's office, I clutched my stomach caressing my baby boy **Preston** praying that everything would be okay. As I lay waiting to be examined I bargained and I asked God to "please please, please" spare my precious boy's life.

The exam went well and my baby **Preston** even waved at us. They sent me home and I was placed on bed rest for the rest of the day. I remember going home changing into my pajamas and falling asleep and feeling a sense of pain. I woke up and had my dinner and ended up falling asleep relatively early that night. The night progressed as usual until I woke up in extreme pain. The day started with me waking up in pain and would end with me experiencing the worst physical mental and emotional pain I have ever felt in my life.

I remember looking at the clock at and it read 12 a.m. August 2nd 2008. I tapped my husband on the shoulder because something did not feel right. I asked him to get up because I began to feel scared. As I was walking to the bathroom I remember feeling a gush of water. And at that point I screamed a blood curdling earth-shaking scream. My husband came over to me in an attempt to comfort me; at that point I could not be comforted. I remember using the restroom and attempting to lay back down but could not because of the extreme pain. I did not know at the time in my ignorance but I had gone into premature labor. I sat down and attempted to use the restroom and my worst fears were confirmed. As I was using the restroom my precious angel baby decided that was when he wanted to meet us. **Preston Elton Anthony** came into this world prematurely at around 1 in the morning. As I sat on the toilet as he hung out of my body all I could think of was my baby, my baby my precious boy.

I could not think. I could not move. I could not see. I knew that I just gave birth and my baby was hanging in the toilet. I remember sitting there with my legs

TIME TO PUSH | 31

crossed screaming and crying fists balled up, rocking and hugging myself unable to be comforted. I called my mother in tears and her heart broke for her baby girl. I called my cousin in tears and she told me that she was on her way. She got on the road immediately. It was a 4-hour drive but she came. We called the ambulance and they came and found me in a spot where I could not be moved. To their credit they were extremely gentle with me as I could not move and did not want to part with my precious boy. As I stood up and they removed my baby from my body, I fell to the floor a crumbled mess. I screamed louder than I've ever screamed in my life. I looked at my husband and he had tears streaming down his eyes as well.

As the paramedics loaded me into the back of the ambulance all I could think of was the intense physical and emotional pain I felt. My baby boy **Preston** was neatly wrapped in a blanket and placed beside me as I was transported to the emergency room. I remember that warm still, quiet summer morning, as I was wheeled inside the emergency room. I was placed in a room and waited for what seemed like hours to be seen. That time is almost like a blur to me and I blocked a lot of those memories out. All I knew is that my precious boy was no longer inside me and I felt nothing but pain. After a while, the doctor came and spoke with me and made me aware of what I already knew my son was gone and I had suffered a miscarriage.

I was wheeled upstairs to the third floor of the labor unit. I was placed in the care of a wonderful OBGYN who was loving, gentle and kind. She told me that she had to give me something in order for me to push out the placenta. As

I nodded my head in agreement, I reached for my husband's hand as I thought it would provide me some comfort. As I lay there waiting for the placenta to be delivered I was in complete shock. I remember that moment as if it were yesterday, Dr. Phillips came into the room, commanding and confident and radiating warmth; I immediately trusted her. She put on her gloves and her gown and got to work. Dr. Phillips told me that she had given me something to ensure that everything that was within me would now be expelled. As I lay there in the labor and delivery unit with a doctor working on me my sense of loss increased. When Dr. Phillips was finished and she looked at me and said, "Mrs. Scott, we're all done, is there anything else that we can do for you?" I remember letting out a blood-curdling scream yelling at the top of my lungs "I WANT MY BABY, I NEED MY BABY." and then collapsing into a ball. You see I was in labor and delivery and I had nothing to show for it nothing but pain. My OBGYN saw the pain and hurt in my eyes and immediately came to my side, grabbed my hands and asked if she could pray with me and pray for me. Through my tears. I nodded yes. My cousin, my husband and the doctor all bent their heads while she prayed for my healing and my comfort. I don't know where Dr. Phillips is today but I need her to know at that very moment her kindness and compassion saved me and provided me with some much-needed comfort.

I don't know how to explain how I made it through that day and I don't remember very much else after screaming. I remember asking God "Why my precious boy and what had I done to make You so angry?" Most of all I remember laying there in labor and delivery with nothing to show but my pain.

There wasn't a little wriggly bundle of joy, with a tangled mass of black curly hair in my arms. There wasn't a hungry or hold me mommy cry to be heard. There were no conversations of joy, laughter, and love that often comes with the birth of new life. Instead, there was a cold, dark, silence. Averted eyes, filled with tears and longing.

I was cleared to go home and as soon as I walked back into my house I could feel the cold dark dredge of depression descend upon me. As I ascended the stairs to my bedroom my heart was heavy and I felt like I was carrying a heavy load. The first thing I did was walk into my son's nursery and sob. I curled up on the bed with the green and white onesie with the little turtles on it, and sobbed. I let out another scream, but this one was different. It was a scream from the depths of my spirit, I liken it to a wail or a deep moan. I lay in that bed for hours curled up with that onesie, thinking about my sweet, precious boy. After a few hours, I walked into my bedroom, took a shower and slept to calm my pain filled mind. When I woke up I remember not really wanting to deal with anything, not wanting to talk to anyone and not wanting to feel, in fact I don't think I was feeling very much I was numb.

Second Trimester of Pain

I woke up on August 3rd 2008 feeling a great sense of loss and a deep sense of pain. I remember being on the phone with my mother who told me she was on her way. My mother sensed her baby needed her warmth, love, kindness and compassion, and there was nothing that was going to stop her from being there for me. My mother, or mommy as I call her, sometimes she lets me call her Sand, took two planes to get to her baby. She came equipped with a mother's love, and Cracker Barrel cheese for her famous mac and cheese. My mother cooked for me, laid with me, and held me as I cried and mourned the loss of my baby, her grandson. She doted on me and loved me through some of my pain. She wanted to make sure that I was taken care of and that I was okay. And I need her to know as she reads this book that her being there provided a great sense of comfort and love that could never be replaced. If I'm ever granted the opportunity to bring life into this world, I pray I'm half as good a mother as she is and continues to be.

My days consisted of the same cycle, wake up, cry, sob, sit on the couch and stare into the vacant space of nothingness. As I stared into the vacant space, I periodically touched my stomach because I didn't want to believe that my precious boy was gone. How could this happen to me? What have I done? How could I bring him back? These are the questions that I continued to ask myself as I sat there on my couch. I began to play the blame game too.

The following weeks after my miscarriage I fell into a very deep depression. It became difficult for me to eat, speak, and be. At the time I didn't seek help for the pain that I was feeling instead, I opted to sweep it under the rug and act as if everything was okay. I have learned that this did more harm than good. You see in the Black community it is often a myth that we have to have it all together. Friends and family would say to me, "Girl, you gone be okay, God don't make any mistakes." I can't tell you how that last line just chaps my entire behind. Those words, though well intentioned, pissed me the hell off.

"What the hell you mean, I'm going to be okay!" I would often scream in my mind, "NO, I'M NOT THE HELL OKAY!"

Word to the wise, you don't always have to offer words of encouragement to someone in pain, sometimes they just may want you to listen, or for you to create a safe space for them to vent. Sometimes, words, can serve as trigger points for people in pain. The last thing anyone wants to hear is about God not making mistakes. Even though I know this is true, I hope whoever is reading this book will take heed to my words.

In true Sheree fashion, I decided I was going to solve this problem. I declared I was going to find out why I'd lost my son. When in truth, I was deflecting and not dealing with my pain. Back then I suffered from a severe case of people pleasing and I could not let them see me sweat or catch me slipping. I would show them, who the hell is them anyway, that I had my stuff together. I say this with love friends, but screw the conventional them's, and do what you have to do for yourself. No sadness lived here, no ma'am, I was gone have my stuff together. I was going to show I could suffer a miscarriage, be of sound mind, sound body, and be happy, all at the same damn time. LIES, and more Lies!

I began to search the inner corners of my mind asking if there was anything that I could do that could have saved my son. I remember one particular thing that happened that pushed me over the edge. A few days after the miscarriage I went back to my primary care physician. As I walked into the office an overwhelming sense of dread, fear and pain overcame my body. As soon as

I walked into the waiting room the tears began to flow I also remember balling up my fists. My husband at the time lovingly embraced me and whispered in my ear that it would be okay and told me to calm down while he was un balling my fists. As they called my name and I made my way back to the examination room the tears fell like a torrential rainstorm. I vaguely remember what the doctor said to me that day because all I could focus on was my pain. I remember looking around and seeing women there with their pregnant bellies and thinking I used to be one of those women and now I'm not. I say this to say that I understand the importance of getting help and I should have sought help that day. Instead I chose to wallow in my pain privately, while pretending to have it together publicly. The thing about pain is that it can be overwhelming and so deep. it is something that I can't quite explain. The excitement you feel about bringing a child into the world and carrying this vessel within your body is something that only a mother can describe. However, the opposite of that is when you are robbed of the opportunity to see that life come to fruition, it is almost like you died within yourself.

After coming home from that doctor's visit, I remember barricading myself in my room and crying for weeks and weeks on end. Well-meaning people were calling and wanting to speak with me but I just did not have the energy to speak with anyone. The pain that I was feeling was so visceral. I always pictured myself as being a mommy. And when you are robbed of that opportunity it is a feeling like none other. I gradually dusted myself off under the guise that I was okay because I was the strong one. I did not seek help and I continued to walk with an immense pain inside my body. I became very, very angry after my miscarriage. An anger so dark and dangerous, cold, gray, unyielding, and frightening.

Third Trimester of Pain

An anger that I hid from the rest of the world. An anger so deep, and filled with hate that when it emerged I scared myself. The catalyst to my anger was that after my miscarriage ten women, a group of friends and family whom I loved with everything I had, became pregnant. I was so enraged and blinded with jealousy that I could not see. In my ignorance I even thought they got pregnant to spite me. I asked God how he could do that to me. After suffering a loss so great, here are ten women who are now being granted the opportunity that I did not have. Again, in true Sheree fashion I congratulated each woman with public smiles, while rage, jealousy, and longing invaded my private thoughts.

I would be left in tears, balled up in a fetal position upon hearing each pregnancy announcement. I would often erupt in fits of rage upon hearing the news of another gift of life, while reflecting on the loss of my son. This was another sign for me to seek help, which I opted not to do. What I needed was emotional support to deal with the trauma of losing my son. What I needed to do was keep it real with myself and others. I needed a space to vent my frustrations, and feelings, a place where I could bare my soul, and remove the mask of having it together. Losing a child in any shape or form is devastating, and I've learned that it's okay to not be okay.

Another windfall of losing my child was also losing my marriage. That's a story for another day but what I will say is that I hid within myself and I hid within my pain. What I did not realize is that my husband also had lost a child and also was experiencing pain. Our marriage may not have lasted but he was a great sense of comfort during that painful time. As I said, that is a story for another day but another casualty of this situation was a failed marriage.

Giving birth to new life/healing gems

Twelve years have passed since my miscarriage. I have only been able to publicly speak about the events of my miscarriage within the last year. Pain is real, mental health is real, suffering is real. I think of my son Preston every day. I miss him everyday, and I wish he were here to see all that his mommy has become. I accept his loss and know that he is in a place filled with love and laughter. I accept the pain of my miscarriage and I'm happy to say, I no longer live in that pain. I hope by reading my story, you see a woman who is fearfully and wonderfully made, a woman who misses her son dearly, and a woman who no longer operates from a place of fear or pain. A woman who takes nothing for granted, and loves her family and friends with a fierce passion. A woman who still hopes to become a mommy one day. A woman devoid of pain, and filled with love, gratitude and light. I hope my story resonates with you. Feel free to contact me to share your stories via email at authorengelle@ gmail.com and on Instagram@authorengelle.

Through this experience I've given birth to my purpose. I know I was placed on this earth to serve as a beacon of light for women in pain. To serve as an example of a person who no longer hides behind her emotions, but who embraces them. To normalize having and showing emotions, while still being able to exude strength, confidence and grace.

Healing Gems:

Through the darkness and pain, there were a few gems that have contributed to my healing.

Gem one: Normalize getting help

Going to therapy saved my life. I found myself riddled with anxiety, fear, and depression, fixated on my advancing age, and not having a child. Going through therapy has truly helped me parcel out the sources of my anger, and has helped me deal with my pain. It is my desire to normalize seeking help, especially when dealing with pain. It is okay to cry, express and have emotions. We need to stop associating any type of emotion with weakness. I walked around for years with misplaced anger and unresolved pain. Through therapy, I've learned it is okay to let it out.

Gem two: Accept and acknowledge that you are not okay

There is an old adage that states, " We plan and God laughs!" I was guilty of planning out my life down to the number of children I would have, and the car I would drive. When these plans fell apart, I did not possess the tools to cope and accept those changes. I did not know how to accept the loss of my son, and I did not know how to express my pain. Through this experience, I've learned to verbalize when I'm not okay, and accept all the emotions associated with those feelings. I have learned to acknowledge and express the emotions, while not dwelling in that set place of pain.

Gem three: Take the superwoman cape off, contrary to popular belief you are not every woman

I know I've probably stepped on some toes with this gem, and that's okay. We are not designed to carry the weight of the world on our shoulders, nor should we be expected to. We are allowed time to grieve, and feel sadness. We are allowed to feel and express emotion. Hear me when I say, YOU ARE NOT WEAK, YOU ARE BRAVE!!! LET IT OUT. Yes, we are magical creatures who possess superpowers, however, we need to learn when to hang the cape in the closet. The cape should never serve as a mask for the pain you are experiencing. Take it off, and deal with yourself.

Gem four: Recognize the people around you who are there to help you, and accept the help they offer

When you are in a time of need, and someone offers you help, it is okay to accept the offer. I'm forever grateful to my mother for loving me back to health when I was down. However, there were so many people who offered assistance that I declined to oblige. I have learned it is okay to accept help in times of great need. I implore you to accept help from those you trust. Accepting help will allow you time to quiet your thoughts, and place yourself on the road to healing.

Acknowledgements

I would like to acknowledge all the people who have helped turn this dream into a reality. There are far too many to name, however, you know who you are. Thank you to Ayesha Pugh@ampdflywife, for your masterful beauty beat, and Marquel Smith Forbes beautifully crafted headshots @ marquelyvetteportraits. Mitzy, thank you for being my friend! Thank you for your words of encouragement as I embarked on this emotional journey of becoming an author. Your love, grace, and wealth of knowledge will never be forgotten. I love you all!

Dedication

I would like to dedicate this book to my mother, S. Wong, father C. Wong, brother S. Wong and my niece Alani. Thank you for your love, support, and encouragement during this painful chapter in my life. Mommy and daddy, your love and support continue to shine through like the golden rays of the sun. I'm lucky God saw fit to make you my parents. I hope to continue to always make you proud, and count myself lucky that you are my parents. Sherwyn, my big little brother, thank you for your brotherly love and for always having my back. My boo, Alani, the love I have for you is endless. You can be anything you want to be, and I will always be here to serve as your beacon of love and light. I love you all with all I have and more. This is just the beginning!

Reflections

_____

_____

_____

_____

_____

_____

_____

_____

_____

_____

_____

_____

_____

_____

_____

_____

_____

_____

_____

Reflections

_____

_____

_____

_____

_____

_____

_____

_____

_____

_____

_____

_____

_____

_____

_____

_____

_____

_____

_____

_____

_____

_____

_____

_____

_____

_____

_____

_____

_____

_____

_____

_____

_____

_____

_____

_____

_____

_____

_____

_____

_____

_____

_____

GETTING TO THE

Endzone

CHAPTER

KIMBERLY
SMITH

Kimberly Smith has been writing in journals since she was twelve years old. She never knew this type of self-expression would carry over into adulthood. She is the loving mother of two boys. She is a teacher. She has two Facebook groups that focus on social work and education. She lives by her saying "There are two answers in life: yes or no, but it will always be a no if you do not try"! She knows that there are limited resources for those who are experiencing domestic abuse episodes. She wants to open more shelters for that population. She has other projects in the works that she hopes will help children, youth and adults become better versions of themselves.

Getting into the

Endzone

There comes a time in a person's life that defines them. For me, the defining time was during my thirties. I was on the cusp on turning thirty, and I was told about him. This young woman that I was, in fact, a coworker with became my mentee. She and I forged a friendship and she entrusted me with her knowing her inner secrets. After hearing about him, I offered advice. She even allowed me to talk to him on the phone while she was seated next to me in the passenger section, so I could instill fear in him if he dared treated her unkindly. We all decided to meet one night, and he was fair when it came to the looks department. His personality made up for what he lacked visually. Somehow, he and I began talking without her knowing. I agreed to meet him for a date. He told me there were no real feelings or future with her. I should have been the person that valued friendship and not allowed it to get to the point of talking to him. I guess I did not value friendship as much as I believed. I stayed the course with him. The telephone calls escalated to coming to his place. He did not have his own residence. He lived with his friend. They had been friends for quite some time. I went out on a date with him. I allowed lust to overtake me. We went to his room. We talked and kissed. We ended up having sex. At this point, I knew that all bets were off as far as any future relationship with my mentee. After the relationship was getting stronger, I called her letting her know.

My mom and I were living together in a two-bedroom apartment. My mom did not like Richard. I revealed my pregnancy. An argument ensued leading to the cops being called. October 2006, I moved out going to live with Richard. Richard resided with his friend. Living with the friend was going well in the beginning, but of course, it became tense. How does it look that two men and a pregnant girlfriend all reside under one roof? Awkward, to say the least. It goes against "man code". Richard and I talked and agreed that it was time to move. We traversed the county looking for affordable apartments. November 2006, we moved out of his friend's house into a two-bedroom apartment which was not too far away from my job. I had a Mercedes, but it was having some mechanical issues. After leaving a store, the car began having problems. I knew that with a baby I needed a reliable vehicle. The nature of my job required that I have reliable transportation. I decided that I would go to the dealership and trade-in my car. I arrived at the dealership thinking that I would be approved for a "used" car, but the salesman checked my credit and suggested my odds on a "new" car would be more favorable. I had plans to call Richard, but my cellphone had died. I knew that he would understand once I arrived home and explained about the phone. I looked at the salesman and Riley. I drove home in the pitch dark. I was able to split the down payment. The purchase was made on the weekend, so I was "loaned" the car until all the paperwork had been processed on the next business day. I was elated; I talked to our son the entire way home about having a new and more reliable vehicle. When we walked in, Richard asked about our whereabouts. I pointed for him to look out the window. I explained about my car and drove to the Honda dealership. I was not able to call because my phone died. I do not recall his reaction, but I do recall he was quietly, sulking. As the months progressed, we talked about needing a bigger space, because our son was getting bigger. We no longer wanted to live in an apartment. We both wrote our bills and put them on the refrigerator. We tackled each debt one by one. When the lease was up, we moved to another apartment, but this time we were more diligent in paying off debt and saving. We began the search for homes. We scoured every inch of the county. Parts that were foreign to me but would later become all too familiar.

August 2009, we found a house in a prime location. It was in proximity to the elementary, middle, and high schools, shopping plazas, and interstate. The house was in a neighborhood of moderately income families. The house was blue, two-story. It had a two-car garage with a door that led to the staircase leading to the door into the house. Once the door was opened, it was the kitchen. To the left was the living room and in front was the family room. In the middle was the staircase which led upstairs to bedrooms and bathrooms. To the right was the dining room circling back to the kitchen. The house did not have many furnishings, but we quickly began to purchase necessary items. I went to stores picking out colors of paint for the walls. I even tried cooking; I was not good at all. I come from being a spoiled child to now pretending to be a grown woman.

The cases became more demanding of my time. I was getting home after dark. I received calls after business hours. Little by little, I was accused of loving the kids on my caseload more than our own child. Those accusations started the beratement. They escalated to threats of ending the relationship to filing for full custody. Over the next six months, I started to believe those threats. I did not want to go to work or go out with friends.

I do not remember exactly when I reached out to my ex. We dated for major part of my twenties. I looked him up on social media. When I knew in my heart that I was ready to leave the relationship, I wanted to see him. We agreed to meet to catch up on old times. We ended up having sex. I had stopped finding my boyfriend attractive. I began to distance myself from him in the house. We had almost stopped all communications. To cover my tracks, I had sex with my boyfriend. The New Year, 2010 came. I knew for certain that the relationship was over. I was so eager to leave, but at the same time, afraid to leave. I did not know where to begin.

On Friday night Super Bowl weekend, Richard, Riley, and I were in the kitchen eating dinner. Richard was extremely quiet, but I did not think anything of it because we had essentially stopped talking to one another. I was seated at the table closest to the wall and Riley was in his highchair. Richard had gotten up to go get something. I walked around the table to the pantry. When I turned with the item, Richard was directly behind me. He stated, "Tonight, you are going to die, Bitch" as he puts his hands around my neck. I fell to the floor stunned and confused. I got up quickly crying and screaming. Richard was holding Riley. I screamed, "Give me, Riley"! Richard ran with Riley to the living room, family room, and dining room. When I got to the door leading to stairs,

Richard blocked the door. He screamed, "You are not going anywhere"! I continued screaming and crying, "Give me Riley; You fucking coward! I want to go"! Finally, after what seemed to be forever, he opened the door, sprinted downstairs towards the door to the garage. I followed in pursuit behind him. He blocked that door. The door swung open. I got Riley and strapped him into the car seat. I frantically got into my car and peeled out of the driveway and neighborhood. I called his aunt telling her what he did. I was on my way to her house, but she suggested that I contact the police. I was so confused and scared. I hung up and contacted the police. I told them what happened. They called me from the Kroger shopping plaza because that was a neutral place to meet and that I would be arriving in a couple of minutes. After brief questioning, they followed me to the house. When we arrived, they instructed me to stay in the driveway. They asked if there were any weapons in the house. I answered in the affirmative. Two officers entered the house, and the other stayed with me. I did not see Richard's face as the officers brought him out handcuffed. Once they were gone, Riley and I went inside. I called one of my good friends who was a coworker and told her what happened. Riley walked into the room. He looked at me, balled his fists, and punched the air. I told my friend that he just reenacted what he saw. I got off the phone with my friend. I took Riley in my arms and held him. We slept on the sofa. I went into survival mode. Saturday morning, I called our son's babysitter asking if she would watch him for a couple of hours. I went to a scheduled home visit though it was the weekend. I did not lead on that anything was going on. My demeanor was purely professional. I was "Ms. Smith". After the visit, I went to another county looking for apartments. I wanted to be close to his aunt's home, but not so far away that I could not make it to work on time. I returned a couple of hours later to the babysitter's house picking up Riley. I could no longer live in that house. The house was toxic. On Sunday, Super Bowl night, Riley and I went to Richard's aunt home because she was having a party. She told me Richard's mother was trying to get him out of jail.

I filed a restraining order against him. I had been in the new apartment a couple of weeks. Riley had a major asthma attack. In panic and concern, I called Richard to come to the hospital. He tried to apologize, but I told him to focus on our son. He asked about my size. I was laying on the bed next to our son. He suggested that I may be pregnant. I laughed it off. In May, I found out that I was pregnant. I was so far along in the pregnancy I heard the baby's heartbeat. I was told that my due date would be in October.

I had gone to Mississippi to my sister's son graduation. I did not want to not honor my promise that I would be there. My grandmother thought that I was going to give birth while being there. I arrived safely back in Georgia. My money was slowly depleting. I moved before I was to be evicted. This time I moved back to Dekalb county. I moved into the same apartment complex as my best friend. I recall once she invited me into her apartment allowing me to shower, eat, and relax. I had not felt comfortable in months. I went back to my apartment with Riley. I was in this new apartment for about three weeks. I was having a difficult time resting. Riley came into the room nudging me. I was still uncomfortable. I turned onto my left side and experienced cramps; the same happened on my right. I went to the bathroom and saw blood when I wiped. I called my best friend. She came and drove me to Dekalb Medical Emergency Room. I called my mother and Richard. My mom met me at the hospital. My brother was there as well. I went to the back and had Richard come with me. Probes were stuck on my belly. The doctor stated that I was having contractions. The baby was in distress. Each time that I had a contraction, his heartbeat would fall. The doctor stated that he had "to take the baby now". There was no time to prep. The doctor called for an emergency caesarean section. A blanket was draped over me. The nerd in me wanted to see the procedure. In a manner of minutes, they had him swaddled and placed him at my cheek. They took him to the Neonatal Unit. They still had me on the gurney. I recall waking in a room. My mom was there. She seemed stressed which was a natural reaction. The nurse came in asking if I was ready to go see my baby. I was so scared and nervous to what I was going to see. He was tiny and tubes were everywhere. I said a prayer and looked at him. In that instant, he stretched out his arms and legs letting me know that he was okay. He was my "champion". I knew that he had the fight in him. He did not pass his hearing test, inguinal hernia, and other complications. While completing a litany of paperwork, I read that at birth he weighed 2lbs 3ounces.

I was released after three days. I went to my mother's apartment. She went to my apartment and packed up my things. She lived on the third floor. I had to walk backwards up the stairs so to take the pressure off my abdomen. I was in excruciating pain. I was propped on five pillows because I could only lie on my back. After about a week, I attempted to turn onto my side. I could literally feel my internal organs shift. I immediately returned to my back. I never tried again. I was given a breast pump. I pumped seem like around the clock and never took a break. My mother took the milk to the hospital. She provided updates. I went to see him. I took pictures. He was so small that he fit inside of my hand. I gave him a bath. When I looked at the picture, I was just a shell of myself. I think at that time I weighed probably 100 pounds.

After fourteen weeks in the NICU, Jackson was released. Not only was there a litany of paperwork but a litany of doctors' appointments. My mother was very thorough in maintaining all the appointments.

I took Riley with me to see Richard. He lived in this slum area. We walked in and stayed in the front area. He put on the movie Transformers for Riley. He asked me did I want something to drink and come to the back. I do not remember anything else about that visit. I do not know the length of time that Riley and I stayed.

I recall after visiting Richard, I had a mental episode. My mom took me to Dekalb Crisis Center. I revealed two possible men being Jackson's dad: Richard or my ex. I stayed there for eight days there. My mother and father alternated days on visiting me. My time there gave my mind and body time to process all the trauma. Upon release, I was referred to a psychiatrist. It was just one of answering the standard question, "how do you feel"? I do not think the doctor was truly interested in my feelings.

The day for the paternity tests. I was on time, but Richard was not. Eventually, it was conducted. The mystery was solved: Richard was the father. Richard saw the boys on three different occasions. After Jackson's first birthday, he never contacted them again.

Looking back, I jumped into everything backwards. I was with a man that made it clear that he did not want children. But we kept having sex.
I knew that he did not want to marry me. Even if he did, is that what I really wanted?

I was hurt beyond repair. My trust, love, and self were violated. My response was how I would live for the remainder of my thirties. I entered unfulfilling relationships. I participated in questionable sexual activities with men and women. I was not in the state of being that exhibited control. It was survival mode.

Over the years, I knew I had to forgive him for what he did. The medications had me in a zombie like state. Like Tupac, my every move was a calculated step. I spoke in an automated manner. One night, I pulled the covers over my head, prayed, and cried out to God weaning myself off the medication. I was determined that this would not define me. The next few months that followed, I was being reformed. I enrolled in a Master of Education program. In 2013, I graduated. I was blessed that event was only one time; some women do not get that opportunity. It was a debilitating feeling that your core was taken from you. Some do not recover or rebound and fall into a cycle of abuse. This can trickle down, if children are involved, to them. I have befriended women telling them my story. They have confided in me that I gave them an outlet to tell their story.

Life sets up the opposing team. The team consists of stubborn bosses, menial jobs, unfit men, or women. It wants you feeling defeated, deflated, and damned. All the papers, napkins, notes, journal entries, poems, and song lyrics became my playbook. That night put in motion on positioning my team. Having talks with God at three a.m., instructed me how to run the ball. Once I got to the one-yard line, the ball was passed to me. I caught it and fell onto the end-zone. I would be defined by that one night. I do not want you to be defined by what you have been through. I want you to know this is setting you up for something more. No matter how long it takes to get to the end-zone, you will get there. The song that played for my end-zone celebration was "Champion" by Carrie Underwood featuring Ludacris. The lyrics spoke about overcoming obstacles. You can overcome all obstacles. We are not defined by the past, but it does give context into who we are.

WAYS TO GET TO THE ENDZONE.

- Get your journal, paper, friends, or computer and jot down thoughts, quotes, song lyrics for your playbook.
- Take heed to your inner cheerleader.
- Find your squad, begin your plays, push past, and forge on to the goal.
- Get local law enforcement involved. Ex. File a restraining order, if needed.
- Research ways to healing.

Acknowledgements

I want to acknowledge my mom, children, family, and friends who have supported me over the years. Your words of encouragement kept me going. Also, I want to acknowledge those who I have met along the way in my life. Meeting you is not by happenstance, but by Divine assignment. I do not take meeting you lightly. I have learned and am still learning about myself.

To push toward the future, one must reconcile the past. One must understand that the past will push you forward or hold you captive. I pray that you will find the words to tell your story.

Dedication

This chapter is dedicated to show how one event could have easily destroyed a person, but the person pushed through. You are stronger than you think. Find a way to tell your story. You will be amazed at who you are becoming.

Ecclesiastes 9:11 "I returned, and saw under the sun, that the race is not to the swift, nor the battle to the strong, neither yet bread to the wise, nor yet riches to men of understanding, nor yet favour to men of skill; but time and chance happeneth to them all." The game of life is on your timing. No matter what life brings, get the ball, and push through towards the end zone!

Reflections

Reflections

_____

_____

_____

_____

_____

_____

_____

_____

_____

_____

_____

_____

_____

_____

_____

_____

_____

_____

_____

_____

_____

THE BECOMING OF

Her

CHAPTER

④

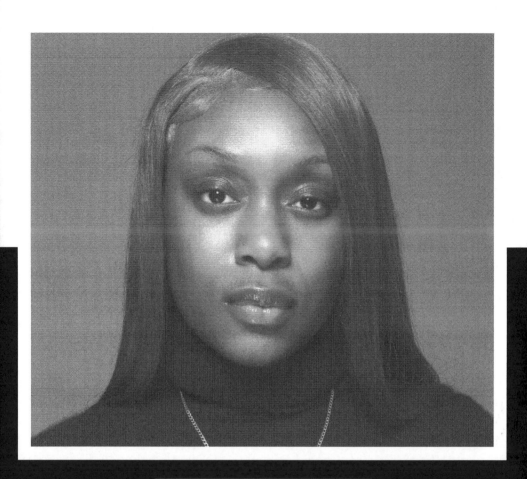

M O N E T
VEREEN

Monet Vereen is a 20-year old author born in New York City but currently resides in Richmond, VA. Monet loves to experience life to her fullest by examining her talents and gifts that God has given her. She wears many titles to include Mother, Author, Student at Norfolk State University and Assistant Teacher. Monet desires to share tips and words of encouragement to help women heal from suffering and trauma.

Follow Her on all social media platforms: @Nizynae 🐦 @Nizynae

f Monet Vereen.

The Becoming of Her

Her

We were born on this earth for a reason. Everything that God has placed on this earth serves a purpose. I knew I had a purpose but I didn't quite know what that purpose was. 2019, I began losing my focus. I had hit a very hard place in my life where things had grown sour with my mother. The dynamics of my life were shifting. At 19, I got evicted out of my apartment, had to pack my belongings in trash bags and get on the next bus to New York where my family lives. To add to this humbling situation, I had fallen in love with someone. I was left to figure out how I could function. Heart in Virginia, mind, body, and soul in New York; I was beginning to have an internal tug of war. I did not want to leave my love behind. He was my comfort at the time and it just felt right to be with him. I risked it all to be with him, altered my morals and changed things within myself to give love a chance. Even if that meant it would leave me with nothing.

At the beginning of January 2020, I found out news that would forever change the course of my life; for the better. I can clearly remember praise dancing in my dorm room. As a college student, I hadn't praised God in a long time, but I knew at that moment I had to praise and rejoice in God because something big was coming. My pregnant friend kept encouraging me to take a pregnancy test because my emotions were through the roof. I was hesitant. I'm still in school. What will this mean? I had no clue where my life was headed but what I did know was that God had something more for me on the other side of this mountain.

Let me back up. I was a pretty focused young lady. I opened my first savings account. I started going to therapy to discuss my past. But even with all my forward movement, I started questioning my purpose. "Without a destiny, why am I even here", I thought. I wanted to end things. But God had other plans. I took the test and found out I was pregnant on January 17, 2020. I was completely floored and full of emotion. A million and one things came to mind: how was I going to provide for my child with no job, what house do I have to make a home? I allowed the opinion and fears of others to overcrowd me and leave me in a state of a tug of war with myself. I was conflicted and disoriented at the thought of motherhood. Should I keep this blessing that God gave me despite my circumstances?

The word to describe that time in my life was lost. My mother and I could not see eye to eye. The father of my child was in a different state attending college and our lovely relationship had now turned rocky. I had to make this decision for myself alone. The opinions of others would not be a factor. I was left so unclear. The enemy was at work in mind and in my relationships causing destruction and division.

In a confused state, I made an appointment for an abortion. All I kept saying to myself was, "I cannot have this baby right now", "what would I give him/her", "I have nothing but love to give."

As I stepped into the clinic, I remember feeling scared and cold. I didn't have a clue of what was ahead of me. Literally, all I had was the support of two friends who accompanied me and God on my side. During my first visit the nurse went over my conception date and began questioning if I really wanted to take this step. The atmosphere of the office was dark, dingy, and grey. There was dim lighting and a protestor outside yelling and screaming, that abortion was an abomination. I quickly wrapped things up with the nurse and headed back to the receptionist to pay for the first half of my procedure. That day I left feeling dishonest with myself because I knew that I could not do it, but I was doing what I thought would be pleasing to others. What I held in my hand added another layer of confusion. It was the ultrasound picture. To me, it was a photo of what my baby had the potential to be in this world. How was I going to be able to live with myself knowing I did not give my baby a chance?

The next appointment date was creeping up on me, but by this time I thought I had my mind made up but I was still trying to force the envelope. I did a lot of crying and a lot of praying on what was the right decision to make. I was appointed for the procedure where you take pills and it is slowly supposed to kill the fetus, leaving you to bleed excessively and have very bad cramps. When I sat and waited for my turn, in the box sized office there were women of all shades, some alone and some with their boyfriends for support. Spiritually I began to feel sick. I went in the back to pay the rest of my money, something in me just did not feel right, I took a step out to recollect my thoughts and discuss it with my friends and two women overheard my conversation. Saying to me that the procedure I was going for did not work for them and that this was their second time back because they were still pregnant. God works in mysterious ways but that was confirmation for me in many ways because I did not want to go through with it from the very beginning. I went back into the room where they were about to give me the prescription and told her I had a change of heart, I was not about to ruin my body with medications that have no guaranteed effect. She respectfully handed me my money and I proceeded to walk out feeling lighter knowing I made the right decision. And from that day forward I started walking and talking differently, praying and anointing my belly because my mother used to do it with me when she carried me in her womb. My mother explained to me as I got older that when she found out she was pregnant with me my Nana told her "you are going to be a mother". With all that was going on in her life, she chose to give me a chance. Despite all the things my mother faced in her early 20's, she would pray and talk to me in her belly as much as she could because she did not want me to feel the emotions she once lugged around while impregnated with me. And that gem stuck with me the whole nine months I carried my child. I knew that it was very important for me to try to control my emotions because she would feel every emotion I carried while carrying her. After I started anointing my belly things had begun to shift around me. I did not know how things were going to go, where I was going to raise my baby, or how I was going to support my baby but God carried me like He always did. Once I stuck with my decision things just started falling into place. What was once a very dark time in my life, when my world was falling apart, and I felt like everything was going wrong, shifted and now everything was feeling right to me. I felt like God had given me a second chance to live because I now had someone to live for.

I would never fully understand why my childhood was so rough, and why I had to endure the pain that I felt. But reflecting back now it was pieces from my past that gave me what I needed for the future. What I once thought would break me only made me stronger for the things that had already been promised to me. In the midst of this transition I knew that God was present but I no longer felt him as much as I used to but faith is like a mustard seed, you may not be able to see it but you have to believe that it is bigger than what you see.

Before school let out due to the Covid pandemic, I had my own dorm room, and it wasn't much but I appreciated it because it was mine and I made it my safe place, my sanctuary, a temple to really tap into what was already in me. That is when things dawned on me and I realized that without God I am nothing. Before finding out I was pregnant I felt empty, defeated, and astray. But every day I woke up knowing that God blessed me with a precious gift and I now feel so rich. Not in the physical sense, money was not tangible for me at this time, but spiritually I was starting to become nourished in ways I did not know even existed. I started to grow on the idea that God was going to carry me with no job, no home, and with me being at school with little to no resources. In Norfolk trying to maintain my education because that was one of the only things that kept me going for myself and my child. I dug deeper into my own personal self, digging out the things that once held me back, the ugly truths that I did not want to look at, and generational curses that weighed heavy on me. I not only sought help from God but also within myself. I began to write. This is something that I picked up on way back when I was a child but it was something about writing my pain on pages that was a relief for me. A way for me to self-reflect and release those things I would not normally speak or share with those who were close to me.

Venturing out to seek counseling while I was still in school helped me prepare myself mentally for what was to come and face those demons I ran away from. The sessions helped me gain a sense of clarity and security that was moving me to a place of healing. I now implement and utilize the jewels that were appointed to me by my counselor at the time. I would often walk out the office feeling light as a feather, because I knew I was not going to be able to carry a blessing with no extra dead weight on me spiritually, even though I was going to gain weight physically from carrying my baby.

During my first trimester I had to revisit things with a sober mind, and realized how my past affected my present. I was blessed to not have to deal with any physical sickness such as "morning sickness" but I was purging out things on a spiritual level. Which led me to have a lot of "healing days". Healing days are the days where I would sometimes cry for reasons I could not find the words to expound on, despite the extra dose of hormones I knew that what I was feeling was for a reason. And accepting the fact that what I was feeling was okay. God's timing was perfect by this time I had fully moved in with my boyfriend and the world was on a lock down for a period of time forcing not only me but those around me to deal with self. The unraveling is what I needed in all aspects of my life, those components molded me for motherhood and womanhood. This is when my inner Eve began to fully blossom. In order for me to really indulge in what God had called for me I had to let go of that little girl that resided in myself. I took that walk with God on those days where I would just lay in my bed and cry. Days where I would have flashbacks of my mother's and I turmoil while carrying her soon to be granddaughter was a heavy weight to carry. My mother and I went to battle during the course of my pregnancy. Being a young woman trying to find her voice, our relationship became disheartening at a time where I needed her the most. But I know now, it was designed for me to walk this journey on my own. I would pray for comfort in those times of need and even if I could not find the words to say, I would try to read the Word searching and looking for God.

I had come to realize that being able to bring forth life is such a delightful gift despite my messy balls of emotions, all my fears, and the chaos that surrounded me. When I felt out of balance I would touch my stomach as a reminder as to why I was here and a warm sensation would flow through me and take me to a place of peace; my baby girl was my sanity. During the exposure of my second trimester there were some waves of consistency where I felt like I could take a breather. I was more than blessed to be surrounded by love and good spirits. I had so many things to look forward to like my baby shower, purchasing my own car, and accomplishing some of my short -term goals that I had set out for myself. I was starting to feel some levels of growth.

My relationships also started to take a turn in my life. My mother and I could have civil and decent conversations to break past barriers that I once thought we could never get through. My significant other and I started taking steps in the right directions as one, and as individuals. I have learned that relationships are like a garden, you have to water it to see it grow if you want your plants to come out gracefully. To get to the root of the problem, you have to trim the hedges off the branches, really tend to the things that can possibly hinder it from growing. Feeding into yourself is also key. I had lost sight of doing so in my pregnancy and am still dealing with it now, gaining that sense of ability to be what I need to be for myself and those around me. It is challenging to maintain a rapport with God, yourself, your man, being able to keep a steady income, and finding a balance in keeping yourself happy, as well as others.

As I would conquer some of my healing days and I thought that I was making progress taking one step forward and then feeling like I was taking three steps back. I would continue to deal with the recurring tug of wars within my life: different ropes, different pulls, all in different directions. Even though I felt accomplished in certain areas I was still getting pulled to deal with myself, I was still being pulled into depression, I was still being pulled into levels of uncertainty. With my third trimester approaching I am worn out, exhausted, spiritually I feel bruised, and I was praying to God asking Him when is this all going to be over? I was ready to push it out. Trying to mentally and physically prepare myself for my baby to come into this world. I am afraid that the spiritual warfare that I had been going through all of these months facing my demons will become hers. I did not want my fears or my battles to pass on to my unborn child. And I was running out of time, because the time to push was approaching.

I remember checking into the hospital room and feeling spiritually I was unbalanced. I was feeling like one foot was in life, and the other foot in death during labor. I also felt like I was unprepared even though I prayed and oil blessed my stomach almost every day, prayed over myself and my surroundings, and continuously read the bible. I waited months for this moment and it was finally here. I felt like the time had come to push her out, and with pushing her out I'd also be pushing out everything I have faced within myself for those nine long months of carrying her. But when the time came I physically could not push. A million and one things came to mind. I knew that I could not let my fears defeat me. Looking back, I knew that it was time to try to dig in myself to push out my purpose. I wanted to feel the pain I faced within myself pushing it out with her. But the pain was unbearable, I caved in and accepted the epidural when it was given to me and I physically felt numb in my legs. I felt senseless in the spirit so I pushed, and I pushed, and I pushed but I couldn't feel her coming. The doctors tried to encourage me but their encouragement turned into fright. I began to see by their facial expressions that something was wrong. I had been in active labor already for two hours feeling weary. But she wasn't coming. The midwife and the nurse called in for help. In about 2 minutes the room filled with assistant nurses and a doctor and at that moment it looked like soldiers ready for war. I was afraid because what I had planned did not fall through in the way I thought it would. That is when I knew I wasn't in control. God was in control, the doctor told me he was going to get my baby out no matter what. He gave me instructions, expressing that he can see her head but when I pushed he was to pull, so I had to meet him halfway.

And that is how God works. You meet him halfway and he will carry you the rest of the way. At that moment I set free from what once had shackled me, feeling her come out of me beautifully. A baby girl came into this world. Hearing her cry and seeing her was so surreal. I felt relieved thanking God for all he had done and continued to do. God never took his hand off me even in the times of doubt, all the pulling and the pushing, the depression, and facing my past. He was making me into the woman he needed me to be for her. I had to be the woman I needed to be to break generational curses. He took me like a sword and put me in the fire. Not to destroy me but to make me stronger. To make me more defined. And to let women know, no matter their age, that your trials and tribulations are your testimony. I am living proof.

Gems to carry with you from reading this chapter:

1) I want all women to know that what helped me get through it, can help you as well.

2) Keep praying and keep God first no matter what. Even when you cannot find the words to say to Him just say "thank you".

3) Praying made me feel lighter in the spirit when things felt heavy on me physically.

4) I want you to know that it is okay to cry, after all, Jesus wept!

5) It is okay to not always know the answer to your problems. Talk to God about it then write out your goals and aspirations.

6) You can do anything you put your mind to, it is never too late.

7) Remember that even though you are a mother you can still be and look sexy.

8) Always put you first so that you can be what you need to be for those around

_____

you.

9) Don't get discouraged when things look like bleak; like there isn't any sunshine at the end of the tunnel.

10) You got this and you already have the victory.

11) Praise and rejoice! Be glad in it.

Acknowledgements

I want to start off by saying thank you to all my family members and close friends who have supported me during this process. To Coach Debbie, I want to thank you from the bottom of my heart for believing in me and giving me this opportunity. To my child and my husband, thank you for being my inspiration on a daily basis. Mary Holston, Monique Holston, Valrie Meekins, Terra Jones and Torri Thompson women who have helped me along the way whom I respect and love genuinely. Thank you for showing me your strengths and weaknesses. You helped me identify certain things and give me advice in times of need and to push me when I could not push myself. I love y'all.

Dedication

From seed to harvest! These pages are not merely paper, but they are seeds in the soil. The seed that I am planting within this book is for every reader to find and birth their purpose. Water your seeds with prayer and watch the harvest that God will bring forth. Whatever it is that God intends for you to receive from this book, I'm praying you will overflow with fruit.

This book is dedicated to the little girl, the teenage girl, the girl becoming a woman. You can beat the odds and live in your truth, unapologetically.

Reflections

_____
_____
_____
_____
_____
_____
_____
_____
_____
_____
_____
_____
_____
_____
_____
_____

Reflections

_____

_____

_____

_____

_____

_____

_____

_____

_____

_____

_____

_____

_____

_____

_____

_____

_____

_____

_____

_____

(PERSEVERING UNDER SEVERE HARDSHIP)

P.U.S.H.

CHAPTER

⑤

R O N E T T A
GAINES

Ronetta is a native of Baltimore MD. Currently residing in Richmond, VA. She is a wife, mother, Minister and now two-time published author.

Ronetta loves to encourage and serve others through the word of God and believes that she has been called for a time such as this. Her desire is to help those that she encounters to heal whole. She is the visionary of an online ministry "Wake Up & Pray!" which began as a phone prayer call in 2012. Ronetta plans to continue her education and hopes to attend Seminary in the fall 2021 semester, if it is the Lords' will. It is her hope to use her voice to advocate for those who cannot do so for themselves in whatever capacity necessary to complete the assignment. Her favorite scripture is Isaiah 61:1-3 and rightly so, as she believes these words were penned specifically for her.

Look me up on ❏ Ronetta Gaines, or Wake Up & Pray, ⭕ @Ronettag2003.
www.wakeupandprayy.com

P.u.s.h

(Persevering Under Severe Hardship)

The pain was unbearable and I just wanted it to end. I had been back and forth to the bathroom at least a dozen times and nothing had happened. This last time when I woke up to go into the bathroom, my mother was in there. She was taking a bath and I told her that I needed to use the bathroom. I began to strain and push. She was kind of dozing off but quickly turned her attention to the sounds of me straining and immediately told me to "Stop." She told me that if I wasn't careful that I would push the baby out right into the toilet. (Abort The Purpose!!!) At that moment, I didn't care because that had to be better than the pain that I was experiencing. What I later came to realize was that I was in labor and the pressure and pain that I was experiencing, were labor pains. I was 16 years old in the 9th grade in high school and very pregnant. I was in full labor about to give birth to a baby, my baby. Push!!! Push!! Is what the nurse and doctor kept telling me. I had finally gotten to the hospital and after a few hours and about five pushes, out came the most beautiful little human that I had ever seen.

Yes, this is the process of giving birth in the natural, but pushing out a spiritual baby is much of the same. There was a seed planted within me, long before I even came into being and even though I messed up time and time again along the way, I never aborted or miscarried. I had no idea when I was giving myself away and participating in activities that were ungodly, of the precious cargo that I was carrying. Becoming a minister was not even a thought in my mind, but I always enjoyed going to church. Getting dressed up, singing in the choir and the food they served seemed to be the best food that I'd ever tasted, but the idea of me being in ministry in any capacity never entered my mind until much later. As I struggled to care for a child when I was still a child myself, little did I know that even then, God had His hands on me. The Lord was keeping and protecting me when I was too ignorant to know who He was. I was lost and didn't even know who I was or the potential that I possessed. It took for me to come to know Him, to get to know myself. When I begin to think back over the course of my life, even though grandma and great grandma both took me to church, neither of them imparted anything into me. They may have prayed for me, but they certainly did not pray with me. My mother was not a church goer and spirituality was and still is not her thing. I didn't have Godly examples, other than going to church on Sundays, and the occasional gospel music that I heard playing in the car or the house. I knew of God, but I had no idea about who God really was. When I was around nine or 10 years old, I would often play church on the front porch with a few of my friends and even knew how to shout like I saw the ladies do in church, until I began to cry, but that was the extent of my God experience.

I became promiscuous as I entered into my teenage years losing my virginity at the age of 13, and as you just read, I became a mother at 16. I was a teenager that enjoyed partying and having fun. I was not thinking about God and had absolutely no knowledge about purpose or pushing anything out except a baby.

It would be years and more natural births later, before I would give my life to Christ and begin understanding and pushing out my purpose. Around the age of 25, I was the mother of four children with no husband. I found myself in a very dark place. I was actually considering taking my own life, because all that I could see were my failures. Even my children, as much as I loved them, were reminders of all that I had done wrong. four children with three different fathers and still no husband in sight. I was completely depleted and defeated. I had not learned that the sin was in the sex, and not the conception. I didn't know how much of a blessing my children truly were, and that they actually saved my life. I was living in the basement of a friends house, with my four children and I was feeling low. I am reminded of Ms. Sophia from the "Color Purple" in the scene at the table when she tells Ms. Celie, "I was feeling real down, I was feeling real bad." I called my grandmother because I knew she was the one person that could help get me out of the dark place and out of the pit of despair that I was in. She was so happy to hear from me, but immediately could tell there was something wrong. She asked what was going on and I began to tell her how bad I felt. As I poured out the contents of my brokenness, she listened and when I had finished her words were simple. "You were brought up in the church and you know the Lord," but I didn't know Him. She also told me to "Get myself and the kids to the church immediately." I did know how to go to church. I got up that Sunday morning and got myself and my children dressed. It was cold that day, and I only had maybe two or three dollars to my name. I fed them breakfast and we walked to the church that I was raised in, about a half hour walk. I was so glad to be there and as soon as the service began so did the tears. From the first song until the doors of the church were opened, I could not stop them from falling. I was like a cup filled to capacity, spilling out the contents until I was empty. I cannot tell you what was preached or any song that was sung, but when the Pastor said the doors of the church were open, I got up and gave my life to Christ. I needed a real change and believed this was the only way to get it.

Things began to look up for me almost instantly. I was on a spiritual high and it felt amazing. I was able to get into a program to get a place of my own for me and my children. I found a house in a nice neighborhood and we moved in. God placed people in my life to be a blessing and they donated furniture to help make our house a home. We were comfortable and happy. I had been attending school to get my GED and the time had come for me to take my test. I have taken many tests before but none as challenging or as important as this one. Me passing this test would change the course of my life and add to my purpose. Passing this test would position me in ways I was not aware of. I took the test on a cold Saturday morning after having prayer with my grandparents. I made my way to the testing site. The room was hot, so hot that I became sick and had to excuse myself, but God. He was with me the whole time and even sickness didn't win. I was a true witness of the weapon forming but not prospering. I finished my test which took an entire day. About three weeks later, I was notified that I passed my test! I can't even describe the excitement that I felt in that moment. It was such a huge accomplishment. Soon after, I interviewed for a job and was hired. It seemed as if everything was finally falling into place for the first time in my life.

It was December 31st 1997, the kids and I attended our very first "Watch Night Service," the sanctuary was packed and the atmosphere was charged! Everyone was so full of excitement as the service began with testimonies. I had never given a testimony before, but I felt so empowered to stand up and share. I couldn't keep how good God had been to myself. I had to stand up and share! Everyone applauded and congratulated me and shouted "Praise God." I thought to myself, this God thing is wonderful and I loved the feeling, but I had a major flaw, I lacked the discipline to be consistent and stay the course. I would go on to make many more mistakes and mess up SEVERELY. I would end up in the same predicament over and over again, pregnant and not married, delaying my purpose even more. But I had to keep pushing even when I felt like giving up. In times of doubt and hopelessness, I continued having this burning question,"Give up and do what?" Suicide was not an option although I prayed several times that God would not wake me up if all I was going to do is fail. But daily I rose on the dawn of the morning because He knew things that I did not and HE saw my future.

Me and the children would move several times. By the end of the year 2000, I was the mother of six, single and relying on public assistance to take care of us. Purpose couldn't possibly still be inside of me unless my purpose was to keep failing and I refused to accept that. I did continue to attend worship service, but my attendance declined. I attempted to join a different place of worship because I was embarrassed about being pregnant after learning to serve, pray, tithe, and live in a way that I had never done before. For over a year, I had practiced celibacy and really began to learn about who God is and what it meant to be pregnant with purpose instead of with another child. That was short lived. I had made God all kinds of promises and journaled about how much I loved Him, but I also loved the father of my children, and my love for him definitely won my affections. In 2003, I had to make a change. We were now homeless because I had poor money management, a lack of discipline and wisdom, so my mother advised (and with help from my sister), that we move to Richmond, Virginia. April of 2003, after my children and I had lived with a friend, then in a motel, to a shelter and finally on the floor of another friend's house, I had had enough. With no direction, no purpose and no money, I had to make a decision. This time I did have some knowledge of who God was, but I had no clue that with all that I had experienced, that I was still carrying purpose inside of me. How could I have a purpose, a God ordained purpose with as messy a life as I had? But the Bible states in Romans 11:29 that "For the gifts and callings of God are without repentance." They are irrevocable, what He has called me to do and the gifts He has given to me are not because of me, but in spite of me. At the time, I didn't know that I had been called but I began to understand that there was something I was supposed to be doing beyond what I was doing for God and I wanted to do it.

I finally married the man of my dreams not long after moving to Virginia and you guessed it, I was pregnant not even a year later. This time however, there was no shame. I was excited because we had done it the right way, God's way. We were husband and wife and I actually felt like I was being fruitful in this multiplying. I found a home church to attend and after some hardships, things began to look up for us, for a little while anyway. I began praying more and even had a prayer partner that I would pray with early in the mornings in my hall closet. I joined in a few of the fasts and saw God do some signs and wonders in my home. But, there was still the lack of discipline. I would start really well, but it would be short lived because I would tire or become weary in well doing. Not realizing that each time I stopped, I was delaying my progress. Instead of pushing my purpose out, I was pushing it back. I was also hindering the progress in my home and marriage. Soon being married to the man of my dreams was like sleeping with the enemy, and I had no idea that a lot of it was due to my lack of obedience. I would go to a few other churches before landing at a place of worship where I felt like I fit. I began singing in the choir, started the Intercessory Prayer team and also began to understand that not only did I have a purpose, but what that purpose was. I remembered one time not long before this, crying and telling God that I was tired of my life, because of how jacked up I was. I wrote a letter to my children and husband telling them how desperately empty and broken I was!and that I was giving up, yet here I was still waking up and showing up. This spoke volumes, because if He had no use for me, why would He bother? God does not wake us up daily because we are so wonderful or just to take up space in the world. He does it because there is something or somethings that he has assigned us to do. To make His name great through us. God knew that I would be doing exactly what I am doing now. I couldn't see in the pain, that there was a plan but God knew. I had no idea that I could Persevere Under Severe Hardship, but He knew that I could and that I would because He knew the seed that He planted in me. I needed to get to the place where that seed could be watered and He was with me every step of the way. He knew what His plans for me were and that it would be Him who'd give the increase.

It was not long after I started the Intercessory Prayer Team, that I knew that God was calling me into ministry. I was asleep one day after everyone had left the house that we were staying in temporarily and I heard my name being called. It woke me out of my sleep and I looked around the room with my heart beating so loud that I could feel it in my ears. After I woke up, I realized that I was alone in the house and knew it was the Lord calling me. I had heard my name called one time before, earlier in my faith walk and I was very much seeking the Lord more and more. Just as with this time, I was asleep and heard my name being called and it woke me up, heart pounding loudly and I knew God was calling me. Everyone's experience is different but I am grateful to have had the ones that I did. My life did not become perfect and I did not get it right because of my calling. In fact, it became more complicated. I didn't even respond to God right away. I refused to acknowledge my calling and I dealt with much envy at those who would come after me but advanced ahead of me. I had a strong need to be noticed and applauded. I needed for someone other than me to see that I was anointed but the truth was that I didn't even believe it myself. There was such a struggle with this thing called purpose. Discovering my purpose made me feel more inadequate, because now I have to be different when all I ever really wanted to do was to be accepted and to fit in. The reality is that I was always different. People always treated me differently and I would compromise who I was to fit into other's idea's and to be included even when it put my life in danger. You see there were no preachers in my family, and if there were they sure were not women. I had no one to share my purpose with, that could help mold and cultivate me. No one to help me embrace the gifts that were inside of me, but when the Lord led me to my former place of worship all these things and more happened. I still struggled with my self-esteem and my calling but I stayed the course this time. I learned to have a better level of consistency because I felt like I mattered. I learned so much there and I am grateful for the experience. God would call me out of this place that I had come to know and love as my home church. I was serving more faithfully than I had ever done before, but I knew my time was drawing to a close. I can't explain it but I could feel myself slipping away and becoming distant. I began having dreams of things separating, being in ministry there on outings with the ministry team but when I sat down and turned around I would be sitting alone. I could hear them but they were now on the other side of the stadium. Wow God! Who knew that you were showing me early on that a time was coming that You would require much of me? He knew. God knew that He would need me to go beyond the level of comfortability that I was used to in order to do what He chose me to do. The Lord was showing me that those who I started with, I would not end with. He was showing me that I would have to go it alone and that "To whom much is given, much is required." is a real thing. God knows what He has given to us all and He will require it from us. Persevering Under Severe Hardship was necessary for me to get to this place. The Lord saw each time that I messed up way before I ever did it, but His grace had me covered even when I didn't know it. I have been fortunate to live through things that have taken others out. God is revealing things to me in this new level of my purpose that I could never have imagined. The ministry that He has allowed me to give birth to, although still in the toddler stages has become a lifeline for me. I love the Lord so much, because He is the only ONE that has been patient enough with me to allow me to see the me I never knew that could be. Part of pushing out my purpose has afforded me the opportunity to heal so many broken pieces of me. A lot of the turmoil in my marriage, which by the way has my purpose tied to it, "I am about to SHOUT," Hallelujah was due to me! God has so much more to show me and I am here for it. I couldn't give up, and He wouldn't let me die because my purpose is so big. He's big in me, and my purpose is not even for me, it's just flowing through me and that's huge! This story that you are reading is not about me, it's for you. Me persevering under severe hardship was so you could read it and be encouraged, motivated and empowered to keep moving forward. To not give up, to push through so you can break through to your purpose. It will be hard, it will be dark and it will get lonely, but don't give up. Trust the grace of God to keep you in those times of weakness. I am a wife, a mother, a minister, an author and a prayer warrior all to the glory of God. Your mistakes don't define you, but they tell a story of how you've Persevered Under Severe Hardship. Give no credit to the enemy but all praise to God for considering you worthy to overcome opposition. Always remember, Jeremiah 29:11 "For I know the plans that I have for you. Plans to give you hope and a future. Plans to prosper and not harm you." PUSH beloved, bring forth the seed that was planted inside of you before the foundations of the world. Don't abort your purpose and trust God to bring you safely through your timely delivery.

Five rules to live by when Pushing Out Your Purpose:

1. Never give up on you! No matter what it looks or feels like, as long as you have breath in your body, stay the course and go the distance until you reach your desired destination.

2. Keep your eyes on the prize. Stay focused and even if you become distracted, get back to the business at hand. Don't lose sight of the finish line.

3. Someone is depending on you. Know that you have been chosen for this and that there are people that you have not yet met, that are waiting on you to get it

---

done. It's not about you but those who you're called to.

4. Celebrate the small victories. Don't despise your humble start and downplay it because it's not yielding the results you desire. Know that it takes time and patience but you will get there as long as you don't give up.

5. Give yourself some grace. None of us are perfect and we will all make mistakes, some more than others. If you mess up, just get back up and get back in the race.

The finish line is closer than you think.

Acknowledgements

I would like to acknowledge myself this time around. I decided to go for it a second time. I am not concerned by who will or will not purchase this work, because I believe that God will allow this book to get into the hands of those who need it. I am grateful that I am pushing out my purpose for those who are assigned to me. I thank the Lord who called me, chose e and purposed me for things I have yet to discover. Thank you again to Debbie LeSean for another opportunity to make "Herstory," in my family. Your encouragement and dedication to women such as myself is not to be taken lightly. You are a jewel to women everywhere. May the Lord continue to bless and keep you as He elevates you for His Purpose.

Dedication

This chapter is dedicated to EVERY person who feels misunderstood and looking for their purpose. Look within and not outside of yourself to discover how great you are. You are exquisite and beautiful just the way that you are. God has made you in His image and will refine you to His specifications. No matter what someone says to you or how you feel, please know you are here on and for purpose. Never compare yourself with anyone else because you are a one of a kind original and the only one that you need to be in competition with is the you of yesterday.

Reflections

_____

_____

_____

_____

_____

_____

_____

_____

_____

_____

_____

_____

_____

_____

_____

_____

_____

_____

_____

_____

_____

_____

_____

_____

_____

_____

_____

_____

_____

_____

_____

_____

_____

_____

_____

_____

_____

_____

Reflections

_____
_____
_____
_____
_____
_____
_____
_____
_____
_____
_____
_____
_____
_____
_____
_____
_____
_____

Black
and
Blue

CHAPTER

BONITA
MOSLEY

Bonita S. Mosley is a woman of many distinctions, sharing three faith-filled lessons taught to her by her mother. Bonita was a Senior Executive Service correctional administrator, who began her career as a Correctional Officer in 1993, and served in various positions, including Warden at three federal correctional facilities. Now, this first-time author shares her inspiration to push herself out of isolation, past rejection, anger, disillusion, and feelings of failure, into a new life and divine purpose. She courageously leads you through the cultivation of her 27-year career in the federal prison system, where she distinguished herself as a conservative, progressive, and forward thinking career public servant. A defining incident in 2018 challenged her identity, values, faith in God, purpose, and ideology. Bonita retired in 2020, provoked by the spirit of God to dream a new dream for her life. She is now laser-focused on her most valuable resources- her family, embracing her calling into ministry, and leading others to do the same, boldly, confidently and authentically.

Black
and Blue

Where do you go when your world as you know it collapses? My mother always told me to have a Plan B. This is all that I could think of in the early morning hours of November 22, 2018. But I didn't have one. I've always been a Planner. A Dreamer. A Seer. But I did not believe that I needed a Plan B at this stage in my life. Why not? I was living the life that I dreamed about. Planned for. Envisioned for my life and career. I was working in my dream job. At least the job I dreamed of getting from my very first day on the job, nearly 28 years ago. Plus, I believed that I was moving, progressing strategically forward in the direction of my deeply held career ambition. My internal calendar was marking time, just waiting for a launch date. I was waiting for "the call." My silent prayer for my career was to be one of my federal agency's Executive Staff Members. I was a career service senior executive in the Department of Justice, federal prison system. But the call never came. Instead, the year 2017 brought sweeping changes to the entire federal government. The agency was changing. While many of my colleagues whispered concerns in private, most dared not to publicly express the fact that the new changes did not include a respect for diversity. Those in my circle could see it. Instead of complaining, I chose to get laser-focused on accomplishing my duties and responsibilities as warden. I loved my warden job, but in my heart I wanted to contribute more.

So, I had reset my personal goals and my vision board to include promoting to an Assistant Director position in Washington, DC. It seemed however, that a series of recent events occurring in my workplace were moving my new dream further and further from reach. I am a federal law enforcement officer. Happily married to my best friend, Derrick Mosley. Proud mother to RaShaun, Matthew, Erica, and Deneen. Since 1993, I have been dedicated to ensuring the safety and security of some of the most dangerous persons entrusted in the care and custody of the Bureau of Prisons, also known as the BOP. Admitting that I am a law enforcement officer and that I'm African-American, and a woman takes courage. In the eyes of a great majority of the general public, criminal justice careers are no longer looked upon as careers with deep respect and admiration. In fact, many now call for the defunding of many law enforcement agencies. There is an old adage which says, a few bad apples spoil the whole bunch. Sadly and through much travail, I've had to reconcile the fact my rose colored glasses have a new reality. In my opinion, the criminal justice system- federal, state and local, police, corrections, probation and parole, judicial, legislative, and yes, even the executive branch, is embedded with systemic racism policies, practices and procedures. I do not believe that defunding is the answer. Instead, our nation needs sweeping restorative justice initiatives to be funded, with competent and courageous leadership in place to implement them.

My upbringing was simple. I was born and raised in West Virginia. My mother was a single mom. I am her first born child, the oldest of four. My mother never married my biological father. In fact, she never even told him that I was his child. Her fear and shame of being 15 years old, pregnant, unwed, and rejected by him, caused her to hide the pregnancy for months. When the pregnancy could no longer be hidden, Mom quickly contrived a plan to get both a daddy for me, and a husband for her. Her plan would be simple. Find a more suitable teenage boy, fall in love, and get married. Well, her plan worked. My Mom married Gates Redman, a young man who loved her and agreed to raise me as his own. Mom was a struggling single mother for many years raising us four kids- Bonita, Juanita, Jamie and Brad, the best she knew how. Now, she is happily married for 30 years to the love of her life, George Jackson. I would be an adult, nearly 28 years old, before my biological father, Paul Jackson, Sr. (no relation to George) would be told the truth. A DNA test later confirmed his paternity. From conception I've been pushing. I share my genealogy simply so that you can better understand my perspective. That is however, a complicated story for another time. Let me get back to where I left off.

I thought I had reached a point in my career where I was now supposed to be more in control. This meant that I was not going to relocate for the needs of the government anymore, unless it supported my vision and my goals. Unless my family agreed to move. My plan for this stage of life was to be content. Contentment as defined in Hebrews 13:5 has eluded me for as long as I can remember. The NLT version of this scripture says, "Don't love money; be satisfied with what you have. For God has said, I will never fail you. I will never abandon you." I believe this is a result of my desire to escape poverty and represent myself honorably in the eyes of God and my family. I began my law enforcement career when I was only 23 years old. I came into adulthood in the greatest generation, the 90s! From 1993- 2001, William Jefferson Clinton was the president. Maturity has taught me that any referral to good days and incarceration are inconceivable, because these were the years of record mass incarceration of African-Americans. During this time however, the federal government was fully funded. Congress allocated billions of dollars to new prison construction, so after the facilities were built, they needed to be staffed. And the BOP was recruiting with an emphasis on diversity. A federal job meant a good salary, job security and a 401k with a pension, and retirement in 20-25 years. My plan originally was to be a police officer. However, a diversity management team of recruiters convinced me to change my plans. The BOP would be my Plan A. The Philadelphia Pennsylvania Police Department moved down to my Plan B. I was preparing to transition out of active duty military service with the US Army at Fort Dix, New Jersey. At this time, I was still finding myself. But, my mother's voice was always in the back of my head. "Have a plan and work it!" In junior high school my Mom and I developed a plan for my life. Yes, junior high school, 9th grade to be exact. Originally, I told my mother that I wanted to be a flight attendant and travel the world. My mother immediately rejected that career choice. Mom's response was, "not that way!" So, with a lot more consideration and research, I made the decision that I was going to join the military. I went to the US Army recruiter's office. I discovered that there was an Army Junior Reserve Officers Training Corp (JROTC) program at Huntington High School. Since I would be heading to high school the next year, I could join the program. Then, once I graduated from high school, I could go directly into the Army and travel the world. I laid my plan out carefully to my mother. She agreed and I moved forward. I then discussed my plan with my junior high school counselor, only to find out that my designated high school was not Huntington High. I lived in the Huntington East High School district. The JROTC program was out of my school district and I was disappointed. I discussed this with my mother and she quickly came up with a solution- request a program waiver from the school superintendent. I did so. My program waiver request was granted. This experience taught me my first most valuable spiritual lesson.

Lesson #1. Ask and keep on asking and it will be given to you; seek and keep on seeking and you will find; knock and keep on knocking and the door will be opened to you. (Matthew 7:7 NLT) Just because a door is closed to you today, doesn't mean it won't be opened to you another day.

Pushing past a closed door led me to discover a purpose for my life in that JROTC program. I joined the US Army Reserves while I was still in high school- 11th grade. The Army's delayed entry program meant I had a real job. I brought home a paycheck every month. I was able to help my mother financially. From this point, my Mom always knew that she could count on me to act responsibly and to be financially supportive for the family. She encouraged and supported every military program I signed up for. My vision for my future widened and I developed a strong work ethic. I successfully balanced school, an after school job, JROTC, US Army Reserves, church and all of my household chores, throughout high school. My two younger sisters, Juanita and Jamie made jokes because I was always running around town in uniform and combat boots. At school, at extracurricular activities, parades, wherever there was a JROTC program activity, I was there. This did not make me a member of the cool girls circle. Being in the military meant no drugs, no trouble, and not a lot of time for hanging out with friends. My baby sister, Jamie calls me a Nerd. I considered it a compliment. I was liked and respected, but too often I was the only black girl in my circle. That's one reason why I was never fearful of residing in predominantly white communities. This is where most federal prisons are located. I am definitely a country-mouse who likes to work, visit, shop, and eat, in the city. Then I quickly get home to my comfort zone, country-living. In my senior year, my plans for the future quickly changed. I earned a scholarship for college. The first in my high school's history, I was awarded a 4-year Army ROTC Scholarship to any HBCU, Historically Black College or University. This "Nerd" had now achieved something special, and my entire family was proud. I had done something previously no one, black or otherwise, had ever done before in my hometown. This was big news in our small town. Now I had several options to work towards my plan. All I had to do was choose an HBCU. I used a highly technical elimination process. First, I eliminated all the HBCUs in West Virginia and Ohio. They were too close to home! I was not going to go to college anywhere, at a moment's notice, my mother could drive up and check on me. You see, this was my chance to go see the world right now. My mother was never going to say "No" because a scholarship meant school was FREE! All I could think about was freedom. Freedom from chores, curfew, the responsibilities of my younger siblings. Freedom from this small town. In my 18 year old mind, my life was miserable. My personal life, that is. Because I did not have one. My mom had cultivated well-mannered, disciplined, and spiritually rooted children who were purpose driven. We were told that dating had to wait until later. The shame, humiliation and guilt that Mom carried as a result of her teenage unplanned pregnancies made her fearless and purpose driven in her parenting style. In her words, "I refuse to let you engage in self-destructive behaviors or associations, so it is my way or the highway!" In my mind, my mom was truly a Drill Sergeant and all I wanted was out of her army. I could see Freedom! I only applied to one university. That did not stop the multiple offers of acceptance from HBCUs with Army ROTC programs from arriving in the mail. Howard University, in Washington, DC was where I had set my goal. That's because in my junior year of high school, I participated in a Leadership Program at the United States Capitol. For a week, I studied in Washington, DC how the government works. I was a high school delegate representing the State of West Virginia. From that moment, the lights, cameras and action of that big city was calling my name. The fact that it was approximately six hours from my hometown made it the perfect choice. All I had to do was get accepted. This experience taught me the next very valuable spiritual lesson.

Lesson #2. Be concerned above everything else with the Kingdom of God and with what he requires of you, and he will provide you with all these other things. (Matthew 6:33 GNT) Just because God opens a door to you today, doesn't mean He won't close it. Stay focused, rooted and grounded in your faith. We are not in competition with anyone else. I have come to learn that "What God has for Me, is for me."

When I got to Howard University, I got distracted. I only completed 2-years of college. But I quickly pivoted and made a Plan B. I opted to enter active duty military service for two years. This eliminated my $30,000 debt to the Army ROTC program. However, my failure to stay focused enough to graduate meant I would not become a Commissioned Officer. Instead, I was removed from a Cadet in the Officer's Training Program and designated the rank of Private First Class in the regular Army. Then I was ordered to active duty, reclassified from my Personnel Administration military occupational skill to that of a Food Service Specialist. The military was not happy with me. Neither was my mother. Mom always loved and supported me. And even though she said she was proud of me, I knew that I had disappointed her. I was a long way off from our plan! Freedom didn't feel so freeing. I took on the spirits of shame, guilt, rejection and humiliation. I spiralled down further, losing even more focus during this period of my life. This was not the life I wanted. It is amazing that even in my failed plan, God's grace surrounded me. God had a plan. I achieved military commendations. Honor Graduate from the Food Service Specialist Program. Physical Fitness Awards. I even received a letter of commendation from my company commander to go with me to my new command. Within weeks of completing the Food Specialist Training program, I received orders for my first duty station- Hohenfels, Germany. Truth be told, I requested to go to Germany. Orders were being issued for other members of my class. Most of my classmates were going to Korea. They were all complaining. I decided that I did not want to go to Korea. I went to talk to a civilian that worked in the designator's office. I asked if I could stay in the United States. She quickly responded, "No." My heart dropped. The year was 1990. George H. W. Bush was the president. Coalition forces from 35 nations led by the United States against Iraq were engaged in Operation Desert Shield. I was concerned about going overseas, but I never showed it. Our country was at war and I took an oath to serve. So, I convinced myself I would be okay. I can't remember if I prayed. During my college years, I had grown accustomed to not attending church and not praying very often. Then, I only prayed to God in emergencies, when there was a situation that I could not handle. Dropping out of college was not necessarily an emergency. My Plan B had not even considered that my personal safety may be in jeopardy in Germany. I was 20 years old. I was most concerned with making my mother proud and maintaining my ability to live independently, and resetting my life. I was never planning to return to my hometown. That, in my mind, meant failure so going home to West Virginia could not be an option. Truth is, the voices of failure resounding in my head taunted me more than the thoughts of war. Germany seemed like a better plan. I was not going to wait to see where the Army would assign me. I was going to make things happen for me. I made the request and it was granted. I was the only person in my class designated to Germany. Everyone else went to Korea for two years, together. After I got my orders, I was shocked to discover that Germany was the staging location for US troops being deployed to Kuwait and Iraq. I survived Germany. Only thing is, when I left, I was not alone. I was pregnant and unmarried. It was time to make a new plan. It was Christmas time, December 1991. I was living in the military barracks, five months pregnant. Now my thoughts turned to fears of delivering my baby alone in Germany. I knew I could not bring a baby back to the barracks. I could not afford to live alone, with a baby, off post in a foreign country. The Army was not concerned about my unplanned pregnancy. There were no counselors. No women in my unit's command to ask advice. Our unit prepared soldiers for deployment. I was lost and had no viable options in Germany. So, I devised a plan. I requested leave to go home to the United States for Christmas. My Obstetrician gave me permission to fly up until my sixth month. I began to think that this plan could work. My leave was granted and I purchased a one-way ticket to Fort Dix, New Jersey, not West Virginia. My new plan was to deliver my baby in New Jersey and figure out everything else along the way with the father of my child. Only problem is now that I'm back at Fort Dix, I am not feeling very confident about my new Plan B. What I learned very shortly after my "boyfriend" picked me up at the airport was, he never planned on me coming back. He had a new girlfriend. I was devastated. My plan had fallen apart before I could even tell him about it. Over the next few months, I quickly contrived a plan to get a commitment for our unborn child, and a remedy for my unwed situation. I delivered my son, RaShaun Lynch on March 27, 1992. I finished my military service at Fort Dix, New Jersey. My son's father and I married in September. Then, in October I was honorably discharged. My plan worked, kinda, sorta. Well, you know the old adage that says the devil is in the details. Yes, the details are complicated and the ending anything but fairytale. So, this story too must be told another day. Let's get back to where I left off in how I was recruited into a career with the BOP. It was September 1992. Prior to discharging from the Army, I participated in a job fair on the Fort Dix, NJ military base. The BOP recruiters were aggressively seeking to hire diverse people to meet the growing staffing demands in several newly constructed facilities. Military bases were prime targets because OPM authorized direct-hire authority for veterans. Prisons are not attractive professions and truly are a hard sell for even the most savvy recruiters. Unlike other law enforcement careers, most people do not grow up dreaming to become a Correctional Officer. So, now that I was out of the military, I had my sights set on the Philadelphia, Pennsylvania police department. Only problem was, so did a lot of other people. The hiring process was taking a long time. Months before the BOP had a job fair in New Jersey, I had taken the Philadelphia Police Department test. I passed the test. Then, I was just waiting on the police department to get to my score and call me to begin the interview process.   I knew from the time that I applied to take the police test that I did not want to patrol the streets. I wanted a job in administration. This West Virginia girl knew that I did not have street-smart instincts. Not much happens in West Virginia. At least not in Huntington, WV. Today, my hometown is a city devastated by the effects of drugs, poverty and crime. The only correctional facility I had ever known about was the county jail. In those days, the county jail sat in the middle of downtown, right next to the courthouse, a couple of blocks from city hall. My Mom worked in the Mayor's Office. I worked part-time in the Department of Public Works. Our town had one black police officer and one black truancy officer. For me, these two men were the face of African American law enforcement. They worked with excellence and were both highly respected. Notably, they lived in our community. Their children attended the same black schools I attended. We worshiped together in the same community churches. I was never afraid of law enforcement, because I experienced the police as protectors of good. I've told you about my mother. She was a strict disciplinarian, so I was more fearful of her than I ever was of the police. This made me aspire to be one of the good cops, like the men I knew in my community. In the words of Tupac, I never thought I would see the penitentiary one day. I did see the penitentiary, but from the vantage point of a Correctional Officer. Then, promoting upward into management positions with increased responsibility for prison administration. I've worked in three maximum security penitentiaries. Three correctional complexes. Medium security facilities, and Minimum security prison camps, too. My assignments have taken me through the valley of the shadow of death. I've come to realize that staff, like the incarcerated, slowly become indifferent to violence, human suffering, and death. You unknowingly develop coping skills to survive in the environment. Too many times, you have to look the other way, or as we call it, "Stay in your lane" to avoid problems with staff and inmates. In 2013, I was first promoted to Warden. Then in 2016, on my third Warden assignment, I was promoted to the ranks of the Senior Executive Service. The highest level of executive leadership in federal government service. With God's grace, my plan was working. This was the career that I had stumbled into after my Plan B fell apart back when I was an unwed mother trying to put my life together at Fort Dix, NJ in 1992. My mother has never been more proud of me. My testimony is that God blessed my broken plan for a family. My first marriage, in 1992 ended in divorce. But I emerged from it with my beautiful son. A terrible rebound, second marriage ended in divorce in 1998. No children resulted, but I was left with a lot of scars. And like Forrest Gump says, "That's all I got to say about that!" But God! He sustained me through that misguided plan for a family. In 2002, my soulmate, Derrick Mosley came and found me in the hills of West Virginia. He was a single parent raising his nephew,

Matthew. At the time, they were living in Fort Dix, New Jersey. The details of our love story are to be told another day. One point of significance is Fort Dix, NJ. This would be the place where God chose to cultivate our love story. What I could not contrive in 1992 through my plans, God orchestrated in 2002 flawlessly through His plan, and His vessel! We married on May 29, 2004, in the presence of God, our family and friends, in Huntington, West Virginia. In 2006 I gave birth at the age of 36 to our daughter, Erica. In 2008, I was again blessed to give birth at the age of 38, to our daughter, Deneen. The manifestation of my greatest blessing, my family, has taught me this third spiritual lesson.

Lesson #3. Give generously to them and do so without a gruding heart; then because of this the Lord your God will bless you in all your work and in everything you put your hand to. (Deuteronomy 15:10 NIV) The foundation that I have built my life upon is this. I am Blessed to be a Blessing. I have learned that You can't beat God giving, no matter how you try! When I quit contriving my own plans, and let go of my Plan B mentality, God showed Himself faithful. Over and over again, God demonstrates his ability to see beyond my faults and give me more than I deserve. Exactly what I need. He provides peace, and not evil, and gives us His expected end (Jeremiah 29:11).

But on November 22, 2018, I found myself questioning God, yet again. It was Thanksgiving Day. I felt like nothing prepared me for this moment. This week, I was hosting our extended family's annual celebration at our home. It had become our Mosley Family tradition to host a gathering of my siblings families (my mother's children). The holidays at our Georgia home provided a vacation-like experience for my West Virginia relatives. I was the first to leave the state. The first to purchase a home. The first to "Make It", professionally. I had nothing else to prove, right? We were living in our dream home. A 4500 square feet newly constructed home. We had plenty of stuff- personal property. We were financially secure. Actively involved in our church and community. And, my husband was just 30 days from retirement, at the age of 50. Yes, he too is a federal law enforcement officer. He served a total of 29 years of federal government service with the BOP and the US Army. Together, we as a married couple were working on our family plan. I had long since put away my individual planning style and thinking by this time. My career was supposed to be on cruise control. But, truth be told, it wasn't. I was doing my best to keep up appearances. I did not want to accept the negative effects of the BOP changes and how they were impacting my personal life. But, for nearly a year, I could feel my professional career in a sort of free fall. The agency was changing and in my new supervisor's eyes, I was not doing anything right. Most of my mentors and good friends were now retired, or in the process of retiring. The 2016 Presidential election brought sweeping changes to all of government. By this time, I had been the Warden for a year and a half. All of the facility's audits were passed and we were preparing for re-accreditation in the next five months. No problem! My facility was staffed with mostly homesteaders. Homesteaders are the locally raised staff who are deeply rooted in the community where prisons are situated. Unlike many senior executives, homesteaders don't move around in the agency. I knew my staff to be seasoned homesteaders who took great pride in their jobs. However, the changing agency caused many of them to opt for early retirement or transfer to other facilities. I kept telling myself not to worry, but there were no new staff filling behind the retirements and transfers. The facility was having problems. I was working 10 hour days. 12 hour days. I am ashamed to say that many days went way beyond 12 hours. Why? The Department of Justice was just like most in the federal government, struggling to manage through Continuing Resolution (CR). CR is the period in between when congress and the president approve the federal budget for the current fiscal year. The government's fiscal year begins on October 1. During a CR, we are only authorized to spend money on "essential services" needed to run your facility. Food and medical treatment, generally are the only expenses we are authorized to incur, beyond emergency repairs. To add to the financial stress, our agency had been without a full-time director since late 2016. The interim director was a career service member, but was not a law enforcement officer with experience in the field. He did however possess the support of the newly elected President and the recently appointed Attorney General- Donald J. Trump and William Barr. Congress and the President did pass a budget, but the President made the decision to implement a hiring freeze and cut staffing in the BOP. Funding was worse now, than it ever was in previous CRs. However, I towed the company line. I supported the agency's decisions. This meant I had to work ungodly hours to try to keep up the appearance of an orderly run facility. I did not let any of my institution's issues make any waves for my supervisors. And I usually never called any of my peers to discuss them, either. Instead, I suffered in silence. In the field we call it- Running Your

House. When you Run Your House, the facility has no escapes. No disturbances. No complaints. Law and order is the focus. The goal is to stay off the radar and don't give Washington, DC or the Regional Office any reason to call the Warden about the facility! That was supposed to be easy for me, so I was not worried about job security. In fact, I believed that it was positioning me to be one of the Bureau's next rising stars. This was my eighth duty station. You see, to move up, you move around. This was the message our agency leadership preached. I was a woman. African-American. So sacrifice was nothing new. My mentors always encouraged me to not be afraid to take on difficult assignments or calculated risks. This most often meant relocating for the needs of the government, to a hard-to-fill facility in a rural community like Pennsylvania, Indiana, Mississippi, or West Virginia. All locations I worked at. Places where minority staff are most often underrepresented. Except in the prison population. The selling point for assignments like this is, it will help your career. You can demonstrate your ability to lead people. Lead change. Build coalitions. The real sales pitch is you help to contribute to the agency's cultural diversity and inclusion initiatives, and make it a location other minorities will be willing to work at. At the time, I was 48 years old. I already had my 25 years of service. Most importantly, I was retirement eligible. My family was done with moving for the needs of the government. Retirement was the furthest thing from my mind. I was content in Georgia, or so I thought. My babies were still in elementary and middle school. I was planning to work until they graduated from high school, then retire at the mandatory age of 57. After all, I really loved my job! I had never once turned down an assignment opportunity. In fact, I had recently interviewed for one of the top senior agency leadership positions in Washington, DC. In hindsight, I know that does not sound like I was at a place of contentment. For some reason, I still could not forget about my book of dreams and aspirational goals. I've modified it throughout the years. It contains the secret dreams of my heart that I wanted God to manifest, just like His word says in Habakkuk 2:2. With it, I have been running. Truth is, I have carried this planner, a gift from my father, for over 20 years. In it, I have written my purpose, mission statement, vision, and personal goals, as I was inspired by God through the years. In 2008, I updated it to include a promotion to the BOP's Executive Staff. This planner serves as a testimony of the things that God has done personally, professionally, in my family and in my ministry. His word says, Delight yourself in the LORD, and he will give you the desires of your heart. (Psalm 37:4 ESV) Maturity has allowed me to understand what my Mom called Plan B, was actually a biblical paraphrase of (Habakkuk 2:2) Write the vision, and make it plain on tables, that he may run that reads it. Perhaps it was before Mom was old enough to understand the scripture. Or, maybe that was just the way that God spoke it to her teenage mind. Whatever it was, I know through my own walk with Christ Jesus, this scripture really helped me to see God's hand working in and through my written plans, my unspoken dreams, and my secret prayers. I could even see Him in my ill-conceived plans. Time and time again, God led me away from my self-seeking way into His perfect will. My plans were now aligned with His plan for Me. But now on this Thanksgiving morning, I was lying prostrate on the floor of my office crying out to God to show me which way to go. I couldn't even think of how to put a plan together. I was in total shock. A human soul that was entrusted in the care and custody at my facility, died the previous day. This was going to be a problem. Why? This was not ordinary death. This death had extenuating circumstances. Allegations of staff misconduct were involved. It was at that moment that I realized I was content. I knew this because I was home all week, and I was not doing any work! This week, I had determined in my heart that my family was more important than my job, so the long hours at work were not going to happen this Thanksgiving week. In the days leading up to Thanksgiving, I had also made it perfectly clear to my supervisor that I was drawing a line in the sand. I took vacation all week long, so that I could be "fully present," mind, body and spirit. Altogether in my home. Celebrating. Cooking. Living my best life. Then, Wednesday morning, my work cell phone rang. Suddenly, in the midst of my joy, immense sorrow covered me like a blanket. The call was a death notification. Duty called, and so I made plans to go into the office, later. I just needed to get my family settled. No one knew that I was going into the prison but my husband. For years, he has always stood in the gap for me. Slowly, with each promotion, without realizing it, I was giving away parts of myself to the agency, while taking pieces of me from my family. Derrick was the first to recognize it. I was always glued to my cell phone. The prison always needed me. Or so I thought. I dutifully checked emails whenever I was alerted to a new message. I was a working Mom. This meant that I was never the first one in the office. But most evenings, I was one of the last ones out. I was habitually late. But, I was up at 4:00 a.m., most days. I was always tired. Late for everything, even though I set alarms on every clock I owned. But I overcompensated for this deficiency. I was meticulous about my professional responsibilities. I made a plan for everything. I worked at home, taking multitasking to new heights. I told myself that I could function on 4-5 hours of sleep. I was always on the go. I even ran half marathons. Running relaxed me and relieved me of stress. But then I then added more stress by working weekends, on vacation or on my days off. My type A personality drove me to take hold of every initiative and organizational goal. Then I made sure my team was one of the first to implement it. But on this day, on the floor of my office, I wept like I had never wept before in my life! I may not have had a Plan B, but I sure did have a line drawn in the sand. I was never going to support the reframing of my staff's misconduct in this death. That was a problem for my supervisors. And at that moment on the floor, I knew that my career was over. But, I was not ready to retire, so I prayed like I have never prayed in my life. I knew that I had to act and I asked God to order my steps. I got up. I dried my tears. Then I drew upon my faith in God and I notified the FBI, the BOP Office of Internal Affairs and the BOP's Acting Director. In great detail, I told the truth about the events I witnessed on the Use of Force videos involving the deceased person. In the days, weeks, and now years since I took these decisive actions, I have felt completely helpless in the fight against systemic racism. You have no idea the actions I received because I refused to conceal misconduct! Nevertheless, the fight for justice is one that is ingrained in my DNA. The year is now 2021 and I am still in the fight to unmask the systemic injustices which occurred in this incident and the 17 months following. Yes, I worked an additional 17 months before I reached my breaking point. Justice is still yet to be served. There is great adversity and hopelessness plaguing the incarcerated. Yet, many men and women impacted by the criminal justice system work tirelessly in prison to rehabilitate themselves. I've seen both sides of the incarceration coin- unrepentant habitual offenders, intent on perpetrating criminal conduct; and unmotivated, disgruntled government employees solely purposed to profit off of miscarriages of justice. Likewise, I've seen the possibilities that rise above the impartiality of concrete walls and barbed wire fences- rehabilitated individuals reintegrated back into their families and into society, collaborating with dedicated public servants, community partners, and faith-based organizations, committed to rebuilding bridges back to the community. I now know that my tears on that Thanksgiving morning were not in vain. I was pushing. Pushing against the evil spiritual forces described in Ephesians 6:12. Pushing to birth the dreams God was placing in my heart, wrestling against everything this unjust system and the world stands for. Dreams I thought needed the approval of the BOP. I cried for a man whom others could not see as human. I treated him humanely and protected his life to the best of my ability. This individual heinously defiled the innocent, but was repaying the debt imposed upon him by the criminal justice system. He was not sentenced to death, and my response was an indication that I had not traded away my own humanity by devaluing another's. That morning, in the privacy of my office, on the floor, I reclaimed my contentment. It took me 17 months to walk away from the criminal justice system that refused to acknowledge, investigate or hold accountable the misconduct, negligent and sometimes even criminal behavior, of my fellow law enforcement officers. In faith, I walked towards the omniscient God who had not yet revealed to me His perfect plan for my future. That morning, I grieved for the family of the deceased, who may never know the truth. And I praised GOD for my family members at home who stood by me through 25 years of misplaced priorities. That Thanksgiving morning I prayed. I prayed for God to soften my heart so that I would not be consumed with malice towards the victims or the perpetrators of injustice. I prayed for God to protect me from dangers seen and unseen. That morning, I walked fully persuaded that no weapon formed against me would prosper (Isaiah 54:17), trusting my future to the God who is able to do exceedingly and abundantly above all that I can ask, think or imagine (Ephesians 3:20)! I am a good cop. And I'm not the only one. I was trained first by my mother, Jacqueline Sue Jackson. A good girl who at age 15 made a mistake, yet she has spent a lifetime praying and pushing her way through adversity to be an example for her children, grandchildren and great-grandchildren. Just like Mom, I am deeply rooted in my faith and know that God still answers prayers. For 27 years I prayed my way through professional and personal pain, trials and issues. But, on November 22, 2018, God required more of me than prayer. He called me to action. It took courage to answer the call. On May 23, 2020, I retired. God's faithfulness has blessed me more than I can describe. Today, I have a spirit of peace about my decisive action that day. I also have developed a Plan B. Only now, my plans are rooted in loving, supporting, encouraging and being fully present in the lives of the people who never stopped loving me- my family. I believe beyond all hope in my mantra- I am Blessed to Be a Blessing! Today's society strives to make law enforcement officers choose a side- Black or Blue. My declaration to society is that I have always been and I will always be, on the side of what is good, honest, decent and right. I am on the Lord's side.

I am not concerned with any labels. I know who I am. I am black and I am blue. I am a Good Cop. I am a child of the most high God. I am walking out the new plan that God has promised will bring to me wholeness, restoration and healing! Underneath my high school yearbook photo is the quote...Lead, Follow, or Get Out of The Way. I didn't realize that I was pushing back then. My future holds many more stories that I could not detail in this book. I pray that you will look for me in books, speaking engagements, and on Social Media, as I work this 21st Century Plan. This time, I have no need for a Plan B. I'm working on my heavenly father's plan. With the full understanding that God created me for His glory and honor. I can never stumble because His plans never fail. (Jude 1:24) Be Blessed!

Acknowledgements

Mom, I dedicate this chapter to you, the cheerleader who has always been on my side. You bravely face every challenge with unshakeable faith and prayer. Then, you raised me to do the same. I hope that I always make you proud and that you always know that I was listening to every sermon you preached. Thank You for the tough love, discipline, and accountability you always held me to and provided me with. The greatest gifts you gave to me were life, finding my purpose, leading me into a relationship with God, teaching me how to pray, and becoming my prayer partner! Through your example, I learned how to get up after each knock down. Learn the lesson, and don't repeat the mistake. Get back to the plan! And to give God PRAISE in all things!

Derrick, Erica, Deneen and RaShaun. You are the family that God knew I always needed. Your steadfast love, encouragement and willingness to move across the nation in support of this dreamer, has given us a lifetime of memories to cherish. We've laughed, cried, packed, unpacked, bought, sold, and traded a life of familiarity for a life of adventure. Your personal sacrifices have helped me to grow in ways that I never imagined. You have been the fuel for this little engine that could. Knowing that at the end of each day, we would all be together, gave me hope to survive the toughest days. Now, I dedicate not only a chapter of this book to you, but the remaining chapters of my life. I am thankful to God that he has preserved the best parts of me for you. I pray that you will allow me to ride your coattails wherever your dreams take us. Thank You for always being supportive and allowing me to have space to get my priorities in alignment so that I could be all that I desired to be for each of you.

Dedication

Dear God, thank you for your unfailing love, unmerited favor, and the precious gift of a personal relationship with your Son. Thank You for holding me together and giving my life purpose, especially when I felt like an insignificant part of your plan. It is because of you that I live, move and have my being. Mom, you always inspire me and encourage me to do my best, be a woman of integrity, and to value family. Our daily prayer calls are a source of strength, and I cherish our friendship.

Derrick, I never knew love like this before! You have demonstrated your commitment to me and our family with selfless sacrifice and devotion. You've built me up, covered and protected me, and given our children a father who loves them enough to make sacrifices. You always know the right words to say. I have learned how to receive them, even when they are not the words that I want to hear. Life with you is better than I could have ever planned. Thank You for loving me back to life after the black and blue experiences and for being the glue that holds our family together!

RaShaun, Erica, and Deneen, you saved my life. Thank you for waiting up at night to kiss me good night. Saying yes to every move. And for being honest enough to tell me that you wanted more of me, at home.

Reflections

_____

_____

_____

_____

_____

_____

_____

_____

_____

_____

_____

_____

_____

_____

_____

_____

_____

_____

_____

Reflections

_____

_____

_____

_____

_____

_____

_____

_____

_____

_____

_____

_____

_____

_____

_____

_____

_____

_____

_____

_____

_____

HAVING THE RIGHT MINDSET TO START A

Business

LORI ANN
COX

Lori Ann has been writing since childhood, but she only became a published author in 2017. Spurred on by the therapeutic nature of written words, she has two bestselling anthologies under her name and has thus carved out a place for herself amidst veterans of personal development and self-help literature. She is also a serial entrepreneur and loves embarking on lucrative ventures just as much as she loves traveling to new places. She hails from Eastern North Carolina, and when she's neither writing, traveling nor being a serial entrepreneur, you can find her reclining for a glass of wine with her wonderful husband.

Look me up on loricox

Business mindset definition

Definition

A perspective that empowers you to consider issues to be openings, and afterward transforming those chances into a business. It is an agreement that everything around us is the aftereffect of somebody having a thought and later executing it.

There are numerous abilities and qualities expected to maintain a fruitful business. A large portion of these abilities is found out, set up as a regular occurrence, reinforced, and fed through determination and the eagerness to develop. Likewise, having the correct attitude as a business person will permit you to bargain all the more adequately with your everyday business since you will adopt the thought process of an effective individual.

Having the appropriate attitude to set down to earth propensities and keep a sound life equilibrium will improve your independent venture achievement.

NINE MINDSETS TO HELP IMPROVE YOUR SMALL BUSINESS SUCCESS

1) Believe in Yourself and Your Business

This is fundamental at the very beginning. You need to accept that you can do it and be effective. Have confidence in your business, item, or administration. There's no point in making a business and investing time and energy if you're not 100% devoted. It will simply be an exercise in futility and cash. Be tough and keep building what you accept is the best thing. Early days are intense, that is the reason this establishment is so significant.

2) Learn from Your Mistakes

Not all fruitful entrepreneurs accomplish significance. A large number of them gained from their missteps and this made them more proficient in handling various issues. Any business can commit errors en route, yet it's what you think about those mix-ups that will shape you into a fruitful proprietor.

Stand up, examine what occurred, consider how you can do things another way later on, and proceed onward. Being a genuine victor isn't about checking the amount of money you have won, it's about how you handle your misfortunes.

3) Watch and Learn from Others

A few specialists in the business field have expressed that learning from others can help you set your objectives to build up your practices and become fruitful. Watching, picking up, considering everything, AND taking care of business.

Envision in detail, design, and execute. You can adapt parts by viewing other effective organizations and business people.

4) Surround Yourself with Good Company

Perhaps the main decisions you'll make as you move up the business stepping stool are the individuals that encompass you. Antagonism is exceptionally infectious and it will be a plague to your prosperity. On the off chance that you need to arrive at your objectives, dispose of the harmful individuals around you right away. It just takes one individual to demolish your confidence or the positive vibes of your business group.

Encircle yourself with other fruitful and objective situated individuals. Gain from them and conceivably take on a portion of their propensities as you continue to head straight toward progress.

5) Think Ahead

Having a business resembles playing chess. You generally need to think three strides ahead and dissect your moves to win. Nobody prevails by anticipating that a checkmate should fall into their grip. You need to think long haul.

6) Be Flexible

Not all things will work out as expected because there are continually going to be different variables that can take you off base. You need to have a degree of enthusiastic wellness to be in the game, you need to expect that you won't accomplish the entirety of your objectives on schedule or at times, not in any way – and that is fine. That is how the game works, and what you need to do is to be open to changes. Having the option to adjust and move with the punches is critical to remain headed for progress.

7) Create A Good Impression

Early introductions last, thus, you HAVE to make the best first impression. Model yourself after others you respect and consistently hear the second point of view on your appearance, either by asking somebody you know or self-assessment (i.e., look in the mirror!).

8) Be Willing to Take Some Risks

There are no certifications in any way to progress. The obscure is consistently there to thump you off-kilter and even draw you down. If you're apprehensive about facing challenges, at that point you'll stall out in the safe place and cutoff your prosperity potential. Dismissal will consistently be there, it's the way you manage significant dismissal. Recall that The Beatles were dismissed by Decca on different occasions before they were endorsed by Parlophone and hit it huge with "Affection Me Do" and vanquished the world with Beatlemania. Prepare to stun the world!

9) Do What You Love and Be Committed

You're probably going to be an effective entrepreneur on the off chance that you have put your adoration and enthusiasm into what you are doing. You may not cherish a few pieces of your work (nobody loves desk work!) however, enduring these inconveniences by taking a gander at the 10,000-foot view will make you more committed to it. Discover reason in all parts of what your organization requires and focus on it. At the point when you love what you're accomplishing you'll work for it, support it and get it going.

Having these attitudes can provide you guidance in exploring the developing business scene. Difficult work, coarseness, and enthusiasm will assist you with accomplishing your objectives and keep your head in the perfect spot.

FIVE WAYS TO CREATE THE RIGHT MINDSET FOR BUSINESS SUCCESS

1) Focus on Helping Others

Consider how you can help other people all the more frequently. To get help, you frequently need to give it first. This applies to maintaining an independent venture in a couple of key ways. First, you need to offer some incentives to your clients and some other partners. When you have a client-driven attitude, you are bound to make progress. Toward the day's end, your clients are your most significant partners. No business can be genuinely fruitful without the help of its customers. Second, giving can help your organization. Building your business organization can assist you in finding the associations that will make your organization a triumph. It is simpler to create those connections if you help other people.

2) Take on New Challenges Every Day

Growing a business isn't simple. There are numerous difficulties along the way.

Moreover, you should be strong. Getting prone to take on a new challenge every day can assist you with being more successful. Try considering how you could drive yourself to be better today. Maybe you can pick up something or reach for another business objective. Whatever your objective might be, attempt to consistently drive yourself to be better.

3) Choose Your Path

One of the incredible advantages of a business venture is the chance to settle on your own choices. Be that as it may, it likewise goes for boldness to stroll a way of your choosing. Think about the thing you are presently doing and what exercises occupy the greater part of your time. What number of them are things you need to do? Are any of them running after an objective you have for yourself? Attempt to continue onward along your way.

4) Don't Complain; Make Things Happen

Life can be troublesome on occasion. Regardless of whether you need to work with individuals you battle to coexist with, or your arrangements don't work out. Numerous individuals default to whining about their issues. This propensity might be holding you back. Instead of grumbling, consider how you could change the circumstance. Maybe you can fabricate a superior workplace or attempt an alternate procedure to understand your objectives. The more you focus on what you can do right instead of what turned out badly, the better you will be.

5) Plan and Execute

In order to have a fruitful business, you need a compelling procedure. Planning is at the core of growing an independent venture. Move toward issues with a plan. When you have this mindset, you can handle difficulties and reach for objectives. The way to progress is tied in with moving ahead and executing.

START YOUR BUSINESS TODAY

Even though a business is anything but simple, it tends to be fulfilling. Figure out how to enroll an independent venture entity and begin today. Learn more about maintaining an independent venture and how personal growth can assist you with succeeding. You might be astounded by the amount you can accomplish if you set your attention to it. It could be a long way; however, you won't ever understand your fantasy about maintaining a business without venturing out.

5 Tips to Master A Successful Entrepreneur's Mindset

Most of us have something that we need to accomplish. It could be to begin a business, create deals, break 1,000,000 in income, or start a blog. Whatever your objective, the fantasy factor exists and once you remember it, you should simply change your outlook and pursue it with reason and assurance.

Regardless of whether you're just in the beginning phase of a business, building or scaling a business, or you're as yet in productive work however playing with the thought of beginning something, having a business person's mentality has different advantages. You probably won't be CEO of your organization yet, however, as the idiom goes, you're "the manager of you." As such, only you are in charge of your life and your vocation.

HERE ARE FIVE QUALITIES OF EFFECTIVE BUSINESS VISIONARIES.

1) Learn to Take Advice

There are times to confide in your sense and times to seek advice. The last is normally a savvy move with regards to monetary choices or decisions that could have major or enduring ramifications for your future or that of your business. San Francisco based SHYP demonstrated a deplorable illustration of neglecting to notice wise counsel about the maintainability of the organization's plan of action from consultants. Chief Kevin Gibbon later said in a blog entry: "Individuals near me and the business started to caution that pursuing purchasers was some unacceptable methodology. All things considered, how regularly do purchasers transport things? I didn't tune in… While I noticed the guidance, in the long run, I can say with assurance not doing so sooner is my greatest lament." Despite having brought over $62 million up in financing SHYP shut its entryways in 2018.

2) Get Over Yourself and Self-Promote

You never want to end up in a social circumstance where individuals murmur to each other "don't converse with her" since everything you do is talk about yourself and your business. There is no need to be disagreeable yet you should be set up to discuss your business. As Brittany Hearst, writer of the top-of-the-line book "Influencer" and a uber influencer stated: "In case you're not recounting your own story, another person will advise it for you." So, it's altogether up to you — control the exchange or read it and sob.

3) Leverage Your Strengths

Business visionaries comprehend that they can't do everything. Effective business visionaries know that they shouldn't do everything. They know this for two reasons, the first being that there are insufficient hours in the day. The second is that we're all normally better at certain things more than others, and we shouldn't constrain nature. While the facts confirm that you need to wear numerous caps, actually if you're downright terrible at math, you shouldn't be liable for finance. Permit some cheap programming and re-appropriate the issue. Finance, expense form, or income projections are not something you need to get half right.

4) Build Your Network

Each business owner knows that the path is generally a lonely one, yet all things considered, you can't do everything. Your capacity to dispatch as well as scale an item or administration, employ a group, or request basic criticism are identified with the success of your organization. Building your organization is critical, however, this is about quality, not amount. Systems administration is overwhelming for some people, however, to venture into your optimal business visionary's mentality, you need just complete two things.

First: Every Monday pick three individuals in your current organization that you realize you'd profit by discussing with over espresso, a concise call, or even by sending an email, text, or whatever. Connect and send them a short message. Truly... it will take you under ten minutes and it very well may be done on your telephone.

Second: Every Friday pick two individuals outside your organization whom you respect or who you would try to have a type of relationship with one day. This doesn't imply that you're attempting to be best mates with Arianna Huffington just because you loved her book. This is tied in with discovering pioneers in your space that you couldn't imagine anything better than to have in your circle. For instance, if you try to begin a blog and compose a book one day, who do you admire that has done precisely that? Who would you be able to discover online that has practical experience in book advertising and advancement? The rundown is as perpetual as your creative mind, so get thinking—you'd be amazed that it is so natural to connect with individuals of impact, fundamentally because a great many people don't try attempting.

5) Set One Goal

Indeed, set only one objective and make it a sensible one. Disregard five-year life plans. On the off chance that your objective is too enormous it will appear to be unreasonable in the chilly snapshots of self-question. What is the one thing you couldn't imagine anything better than to accomplish or achieve in the following ninety days? Only one! At that point create a rundown of the multitude of things you can think about that need to end up supporting that objective. Pick one of them and start it today. It doesn't make a difference how little it very well may be, the very act of beginning has power in itself and will drive you forward.

The excellence of the business person's attitude is that it doesn't need any conventional preparation or unique learning. It is tied in with utilizing natural practices and gifts that we have and applying a little self-restraint. Thus, paying little heed to what stage you're at, or what venture or dream you are on the cliff of starting with, you are your own supervisor and you are the only one holding you back.

Reflections

_____

_____

_____

_____

_____

_____

_____

_____

_____

_____

_____

_____

_____

_____

_____

_____

_____

_____

_____

_____

_____

Reflections

ARE YOU TRYING TO

PUSH OUT YOUR BUSINESS IDEAS?

MAYBE THIS WILL HELP

WHAT **BUSINESS CONCEPTS** DO YOU HAVE?

CONCEPT 1

_____
_____
_____
_____

CONCEPT 2

_____
_____
_____
_____

CONCEPT 3

_____
_____
_____
_____

CONCEPT 4

_____
_____
_____
_____

CONCEPT 5

_____
_____
_____
_____

CONCEPT 6

_____
_____
_____
_____

The Foundation of Your Business

The Foundation of any business is **STRATEGIC** planning

What is the mission of your business?

The Mission Statement answers the question: why? Why do you exist? What is your goal? What service will you provide?

What is the vision of your business?

The vision Statement outlines the future objective of your company. Where do you want to be in 5 years? How will you get there. Get strategic!

The Mission and Vision are essential in helping your company define it's purpose and thus are critical to strategic planning. Both statements allow you to stay goal oriented. Adhering to both statements allow you to stay focused and remind you to only work on those things that support your 2 statements!

CORE VALUE

Core Values reflect those things that your company believe in. They are your company's guiding principles, beliefs and philosophies. Try limiting your core values to 7! Feel free to google "Core Values" and tons of sites will pop up. From the lists that you review, list your top 7 and why they're important below!

BUSINESS PLAN

A Business Plan can take on many forms and look different according to your particular venture.

1 ## EXECUTIVE SUMMARY
This is your elevator pitch! It may include the company background and why you got started.

2 ## BUSINESS STRUCTURE
This is your elevator pitch! It may include the company background and why you got started.

3 ## MARKET STRATEGIES
This section talks about your competition and what you bring to the market. Testimonials help here too.

4 ## PERSONNEL
Resumes and your staff background help explain how your expertise helps reach the company's goals.

HONORABLE MENTION

Financial documents are also very helpful to your business plan.They provide your forward-looking projections.

TO DO LIST

☐ 1. Business Name:_____

☐ 2. Business Structure: LLC, INC, etc._____

☐ 3. Check with your state's Corporation Commission to get registered.

☐ 4. Do you need an EIN? Visit IRS.GOV and obtain a FREE one.

☐ 5. Do you need business licenses? Apply as necessary

☐ 6. Business Bank Account. Check with your financial institution to see what paperwork they require to set up your account.

☐ 7. Complete Your Business Plan

☐ 8. Business Location. Designate a space at home or begin checking out locations for your new venture.

☐ 9. Other _____

☐ 10. Other _____

Reflections

_____
_____
_____
_____
_____
_____
_____
_____
_____
_____
_____
_____
_____
_____
_____
_____
_____
_____
_____
_____